JOSEPH
of
Nazareth

Federico Suarez

JOSEPH
of Nazareth

SCEPTER

London - New York

Published in England by SCEPTER LTD., 1 Leopold Road, London W5 3PB and in the United States by SCEPTER PRESS INC., 481 Main Street, New Rochelle, N.Y. 10801.

First published in English in 1984, this is a translation of *José, Esposo de María*, 1982, Madrid.

Nihil Obstat: A. Cowan (Censor)
Imprimatur: Mgr. J. Crowley V.G.
Westminster, 23 May 1984
The *Nihil Obstat* and *Imprimatur* are a declaration that a book or pamphlet is considered to be free from moral or doctrinal error. It is not implied that those who have granted the *Nihil Obstat* and *Imprimatur* agree with the contents, opinions or statements expressed.

The cover illustration, by kind permission of the Detroit Institute of Arts, is *The Flight into Egypt* by Bartolomé Esteban Murillo (1617-1682).

Typeset by Vera-Reyes, Inc. (Manila) and printed in England by Haynes Cannon Ltd, Wellingborough.

CONTENTS

CONTENTS

PROLOGUE

If I were a person writing with authority, I would gladly describe, at greater length and in the minutest detail, the favours which this glorious saint has granted to me and to others. But in order not to do more than I have been commanded I shall have to write about many things briefly, much more so than I would wish, and at unnecessarily great length about others: in short, I must act like one who had little discretion in all that is good. I only beg, for the love of God, that anyone who does not believe me will put what I say to the test, and he will see by experience what great advantages come from his commending himself to this glorious patriarch and having devotion to him. Those who practise prayer should have a special devotion to him always. I do not know how anyone can think of the Queen of the Angels, during the time that she suffered so much with the Child Jesus, without giving thanks to Saint Joseph for the way he helped them. If anyone cannot find a master to teach him how to pray, let him take this glorious saint as his master and he will not go astray. May the Lord grant that I have not erred in venturing to speak of him; for though I make public acknowledgment of devotion to him, in serving and imitating him I have always failed. He was true to his own nature when he cured my paralysis and gave me the power to rise and walk; and I am following my own nature in using this favour so ill.

SAINT TERESA OF JESUS
(Life, chapter 6)

FOREWORD

It isn't easy to write reliably on Saint Joseph, the last of the patriarchs, the craftsman of Nazareth and the spouse of Our Lady. Every historian knows that without sources history is impossible. One cannot attain it through simple conjecture. Once a few facts are available it is possible to go a little farther and trace a sketch enriched with the help of an appropriate setting. But this can never become even a brief biography.

However, to write not on Saint Joseph, but on themes concerning the saint or with regard to him, is different. For one is not attempting a biography but a reflection. Or, if you like, a meditation. It is not a reconstruction of a life but a series of considerations derived from a few facts, which are not explicit but are inferred.

The facts which are developed are very important. St Thomas More, in a meditation on the Agony of Christ which he wrote as a prisoner in the Tower of London, says that it is no mere coincidence that one or other name (which could have been omitted) appears in the Gospel. That it is there indicates something. "Not one syllable," he continues, "in a writing inspired by the Holy Spirit can be considered vain or superfluous." It is not possible to hold that in the Scriptures there is anything fortuitous.

And this is something we ought to be very keenly aware of. St Paul says: "All Scripture is inspired by God and profitable for teaching" (II Tim 3:16). When the Gospels then speak of Saint Joseph or in some way relate this or that to him, the statement is there by the design of the Holy Spirit, with neither deficiency nor excess, for our edification. And in these facts, even if they are implicit, there is a lesson for us.

The devotion Mgr. Escrivá de Balaguer had for the holy patriarch led him to sketch this terse and penetrating portrait: "He is an ordinary man, a family man, a worker who earned his living with his hands"[1]. But isn't this something that can be said of very many people? And isn't this to say that holiness — for Joseph is a great saint — is accessible in the most ordinary and everyday occupations? And if this is the case, cannot contemplation of the Gospel insofar as it refers in one way or other to this person (who, humanly speaking, is so much at our own level), reveal to us the secret of sanctity in work and in the fulfilment of one's duties?

It is clear that a theme such as this will appear, and with good reason, to be presumptuous. Nevertheless, some words from St John of Avila exonerating his own boldness can, perhaps, if not justify, at least excuse this work. "Just as everything said in praise of the Blessed Virgin, as St Jerome says, results in honour of Our Lord Jesus Christ, her Blessed Son, so everything said in favour of Saint Joseph results in honouring Our Lord Jesus Christ, who honoured him with the title of father, and in honouring Mary, whose truest and most chaste spouse he was. Our Lord wishes his holy tutor to be honoured, and Our Lady wants us to speak well of her spouse. Both He and she will be grateful and will reward it. And since it is for the honour of God and also to win such a reward, we will begin our history in praise of this glorious saint, spouse of the Virgin."

---

[1] *In Joseph's Workshop,* a homily included in *Christ is Passing By,* (no. 39). Henceforth, so as not to multiply footnotes unnecessarily (for this is neither a work of research nor an erudite one) all quotations from this author are from the same homily unless otherwise indicated. Those from St John Chrysostom are from his *St Matthew,* and those from St Augustine are from *Sermon 51.*

She, the Most Blessed Mother of God, would like to help us discover the greatness of him whom she loved so much and whom the Holy Spirit called 'the just man'. And she will help us imitate his faithfulness, a virtue so necessary in these times which are so little inclined to value it.

F.S.

Publishers' Acknowledgements

The Publishers wish to thank the translation unit headed by Ives Mascarenhas and Patrick Kearns who revised the whole script. The Prologue is taken from E. Allison Peers' translation of *The Complete Works of St Teresa of Jesus* (1946) by kind permission of Messrs Sheed & Ward.

1

The Figure of Joseph

There are saints whose heroic stature and exceptional virtues are almost dramatically conspicuous. Their sanctity arouses admiration and stirs up a burning desire to imitate them. Pretty obviously Joseph does not belong to this category. He is more appropriately to be included in the long and less colourful list of men and women who, if by some accident they happen to be noticed at all, will hardly incline an observer to give them a second glance. They are the modern world's 'faceless men', those who may never be distinguished from the anonymous crowd because they are so well blended into the unremarkable generality of men. There is not the least unusual detail about them to attract our attention. And it is not from such a class of men that archetypes emerge for us to aspire to.

Joseph passes through the Gospel without our hearing him utter as much as a single word. He is not on record as having written a single line. None of the things he did seem to have exceeded the limits of the most common actions. He appears to have been — to use an overworked modern expression — a man without a message.

Clearly all this is what appears at first sight: what *appears* certainly, but, in an unmistakable sense, what nevertheless *is* — for the impression is a true one. It does correspond to reality. Saint Joseph was no scintillating star. But is brilliance in itself essentially valuable? Is renown the most reliable measure of worth?

Neither does Joseph seem to have left for posterity any legacy. An Archimedes, an Aquinas, a Michaelangelo, an Edison — each has significantly advanced the common patrimony of humanity. The twentieth century consequences of their contributions are beyond calculation. We are compelled to admit that Joseph has not put us in his debt to the extent of so manifestly requiring our expression of gratitude. Nor was he interested in the plaudits of ages to come. From what we know of him, it does not seem to be a question over which he would have lost any sleep or have become embroiled in worry.

His figure could, in a certain sense then, appear to the eyes or in the estimation of some as that of the man-in-the-street, so ordinary that little could usefully be said of him to those who would come after. Those who think in this way are perhaps to be found among the regretably too many who nowadays employ in their judgement inadequate criteria having only short term values. They make their assessments by following some conventional guidelines which are based more on appearance than on reality, more on popular opinion than on absolute and true values. In other words, more importance is placed on worldly rankings than on supernatural criteria. People are in consequence judged not for what they are, not even for what good they have done but only by certain 'achievements' which, it has been previously decided, are to be classified as meritorious or worth recognising with acclaim.

It is not surprising then, that using such fashionable criteria with little or no supernatural dimension to them and in general lacking in any depth, the figure of Joseph is a little hazy and indistinct, and apparently deficient in personality. Men of our time do not see the figure of Joseph as sufficiently interesting to consider it worth a more detailed examination. With such criteria an unexciting man, a village craftsman who never seems to have made an utterance of any importance, who never made anything worth preserving, could be quite respectable and a good man. But life is too short for us to reflect on all the good men there have been in the world. There are more urgent, more useful, more necessary and more important things to get on with.

But He Was Selected by God

By the world's standards, that God chose this man to take custody of the two greatest treasures — Jesus and Mary — who have ever been on earth, does not count for much. This can certainly be one of the reasons which allows one confidently to assert that such criteria are of this world and consequently superficial. For this very reason such criteria will always fall short of practical usefulness for a christian who really is what his name indicates — a *disciple* of Christ. A disciple of Christ can never accept anything at its face value. Such value is of no use, for what one needs is the knowledge of its real value.

And the real value of created things, whatever they be, their truest and deepest value, is closely related to God, with Christ, with the supernatural world and with revelation.

For a christian who believes in Jesus Christ, who believes that Jesus *is* true God and true Man, that God was to choose Joseph as Our Lady's spouse and the legal father of Jesus, is sufficient reason for him to feel that perhaps Joseph was not, after all, such an ordinary man as he seems. God had chosen him — in fact he had created him — to undertake one of the most difficult and responsible missions which have ever been entrusted to man.

Perhaps the consideration of Joseph's selection for this special mission can serve as a starting point for a series of reflections. At the end of these our esteem and our respect for this saint will have grown considerably. To all appearances he does not seem to have been more than a good man, a personality dim but of uncommon richness. This man, who never uttered a single word in his passage through the Gospel, gives us a lesson of deafening eloquence. This man who did not write a single line, nor left us a single thought, teaches us such profound lessons that it is doubtful whether even a small proportion of the men of today will be capable of perceiving this. For contemporary man feels little desire for reflection. And work, business, hurry and the constant desire for (or displeasure at) change leave him little time either.

An attempt to compose a biography of Joseph of Nazareth would be rash. One cannot have a biography (no less than a personal history) without the requisite data. What the Gospels give us is very limited. They are too poor to reconstruct a life. They are, on the other hand, very significant and more than enough to give rise to a serious and respectful deliberation. But not to just any consideration, for this is not merely an intellectual exercise. It is, moreover, an exercise in piety, a reflection in the light of faith and based on information and events which are part of revelation. For some facts have certainly been written down — for our edification and use.

Christian criterion allows us to see such facts with an extra dimension — that of supernatural vision. Joseph then appears as the person most united (after Mary) to the Blessed Trinity. On Joseph fell, in the words of Pius IX, "the mission of guarding the virginity and sanctity of Mary; he being the only man called to share in the knowledge of the great mystery hidden for centuries, his mission was to cooperate in the divine Incarnation and in the salvation of the human race". Doubtless, his was a highly delicate mission and one of great responsibility. It was fraught with difficulties because of the exceptional qualities of Mary (full of grace, Mother, Daughter and Spouse of the same God) and because the Child whom he had to watch over was the Creator of the world and his Master. By any reckoning, and even to a mediocre mind, it is clear that he was going to be inferior to the persons subordinated to him. And how difficult it is to direct those who are superior to us! What tremendous difficulties are entailed when resolutions have to be taken affecting those people whom we know to be more intelligent, more capable, better prepared and more sensitive than ourselves! Unless there is a deeply rooted humility, it is almost inevitable that a complex of inferiority will lead to resentment or that timidity will result in one resorting to subterfuges to mask it.

Saint Joseph never had to overcome any such complex. There are some who find themselves less important than they would like to be, and this makes them bitter and aggressive. Or perhaps they try to disguise a run-of-the-mill personality by developing an appearance — cultivating an image, as they say nowadays. This, they feel, will make them seem better to others than they really are; now they will be appreciated for what they seem to be, for they would not be noticed for what they are.

Nothing of the sort happens with Joseph. His figure carries the stamp of authenticity, of one who accepts himself as he is. There is not in him the slightest note of falsity. There is nothing devious, politic or abrasive about him, nothing at all discordant or merely assumed in his manner. Free from affectation, he shows no sign of concern for what others may think or say about him. His 'image' is of no importance. He has no desire to be, or to appear to be, other than he is.

A Model for Us, Ordinary People

Nonetheless, from another point of view the task entrusted to him was well within his reach since, as St John Chrysostom says, what he was asked to do was what is required of any father of a family — to maintain them and to shepherd their growth and education. He was, however, immersed in the mystery of Redemption, alongside the two principals. He was to limit himself to a role less than secondary, in itself having no direct part in the Redemption. It was no part of his work to participate actively in forming the New Covenant, as it would be, for example, in the case of the Apostles. And he had to carry out the work entrusted to him with precision, without regard to any kind of personal ambition, without becoming disheartened or frustrated, or hurt through pride, and without departing in the slightest degree from his assigned place and particular business. What is certain is that all this would call for qualities not commonly found among men.

Such natural and supernatural qualities, scarcely visible to the superficial glance and hidden completely from minds preoccupied with distractions, gradually become clear to the eyes of those who, through reflection, study in depth the few but significant facts given us by the Gospels about one who has been perceptively called "God's right hand man". All of which gives the lie to that first indistinct impression we might have formed of a very ordinary fellow. The real and true figure of Joseph becomes more visible when such vagueness is seen to be without relevance. Joseph is shown to be the archetypal figure of what we all ought to be — with a difference, naturally. The majority of mankind can look on Joseph as an exemplar, perhaps precisely because our lives do not seem to surpass the most common general standards of ordinariness, and because our actions are routine without outstanding significance. Just as the Gospel permits us to see him, we recognise the same figure who is summarised in the few but extremely expressive words of Mgr J. Escrivá: "He did exactly what Our Lord wanted him to do, in each and every event that went to make up his life. That is why Scripture praises Joseph as 'a just man' (Matt 1:19)". It is not something that can be said of most of us.

The figure of Joseph, then, is an incentive God has given us to stir up our hope. For if we are not going to be anything other than ordinary men, with nothing special to distinguish us from the rest, with none of those qualities that would lift us head and shoulders above our fellow-men, we can still aspire to something a million miles from mediocrity. We may have felt destined to such insignificance because we lacked exceptional abilities. Fortunately for us, God uses a very different yardstick from the one we men are accustomed to. It is not a matter of talents and aptitudes outside of the ordinary, but of making the best of what abilities we have been endowed with. What matters is that we carry out well our own task, the assignment each one has in God's plan, following one's own vocation in the place where it is to be fulfilled. This job is to be properly done, completed, well finished, so that nothing is lacking or superfluous, without either deficiency or excess.

It is not necessary for all of us to shine before men; they do not even need to know of our existence. For neither prominence nor lack of it is of the least importance. It is sufficient merely to carry out the little, commonplace, almost banal duties of each day with love and humility, and with the intention of pleasing God. In his eyes this is what gives witness to and proclaims the intrinsic qualities of man. To sum up, we recall that "no man is worthless to God. All of us are called to share in the kingdom of heaven — each with his own vocation: in his home, his work, his civic duties and the exercise of his rights" (Mgr Escrivá). And it is Joseph, the last of the patriarchs, who shows us how, in following this way, any one of us can come to be a great saint.

2

A Quiet Man

What first attracts our attention when we begin to study the figure of Saint Joseph is, in a certain sense, a negative feature. He passes through the Gospel like a shadow, unnoticed, soundlessly and without creating the slightest ripple. In fact he does not say a word at all.

St Matthew introduces him to us at the beginning of his narrative as an anxious man, trying to find an honourable and just way out of a serious dilemma in which he has found himself. But he does so in silence. He allows no one else to intervene in a private matter which is nevertheless not his concern alone. He cannot communicate it without risking harm to another person. He is a man who, alone with God and his own conscience, examines a situation with serenity. Without grumbling, without seeking the support of others on whom he can unburden some of his responsibility, he faces circumstances and carries the consequences of his own decision with calm lucidity.

As soon as Cæsar Augustus' edict is made public, without either complaint or delay he leaves Nazareth with his spouse in order to register at Bethlehem. There is not a whisper of anxiety, nor any sign of his humiliation at not finding in the city of David a roof for Our Lady who is about to give birth. Nor does he offer a single excuse at not being able to provide for her anything else but a manger in a cave with, perhaps, just a little clean straw. There, without a comment, in silence, he observes the shepherds file past, sees the vision of angels in the night, and witnesses the homage paid to the Child and its Mother.

He goes to and returns from Egypt without seeking a single explanation for the mysterious commands that prompted those arduous journeys; and without any more explanation he takes the road to Galilee and to Nazareth. Some more years ensue in that remote corner, with a further, even more profound silence, if that were possible. Even when he could have spoken, when he discovered Jesus in the temple after three days of unbearable anguish, he steps to one side. He lets Her, the Mother, speak, and she asks the questions which have to be asked. After this he disappears from the Gospel and quietly moves into oblivion. We are not told as much as a word about his death. He is remembered just once, and even then not by name; in Nazareth, admiring the wisdom of Jesus, his fellow villagers exclaim "Is this not the son of the craftsman?" (Matt 13:55).

Joseph had nothing to say to us. Nor would anything routine he said to others have been of compelling interest to us in any case. But there are different

kinds of silence. Clearly Joseph's silence is not the
result of a withdrawn, uncommunicative sort of
half-life shared with a vague and inarticulate people,
or lived out in an epoch of such bland and colourless
mediocrity that there was nothing to be spoken of.
Quite the contrary. The people and the era are
without doubt not only notable but, in a truly remarkable way, unique. So sharply and distinctly do
they stand out in history that they are incomparable
and unrepeatable. Never in the entire history of the
world will there be a similar moment, nor will anyone ever live so closely with the divine as then. For
Earth, the planet God made to be inhabited by men,
is never again to shelter the Only Begotten Son of
God made Man. Nor is it to contemplate ever again a
creature like the Blessed Virgin Mary. In no other
period of recorded or future history will there be
repeated that totally unprecedented phenomenon of
a dozen unknown, simple and uncultured men, rural
villagers with no special vision or heroic dynamism
and lacking in the most elementary qualities requisite for leadership or excellence, who initiated a
transformation so staggering that the world will
never know another like it.

The silence of Joseph is not due to the historical
setting, the people or the era. We know as we leaf
through the pages of the Gospels, that not one
spoken word of his has been preserved for us. But
the reason for this we do not know. And however
many guesses, theories or explanations we would like
to give to account for this fact, they would lack
certainty, pious and useful though they might be.
What is not uncertain, on the other hand, is the fact
which has just been noted — in the Gospel *Joseph
says absolutely nothing*. And from this we can deduce more useful consequences for our ordinary life

than we could from many a reflection upon the reasons for his silence.

A Silence Which Inspires

Ernest Heller writes that "this man, enshrouded in silence, inspires silence." But Joseph's is not an empty silence. It is not the simple absence of words and of thought, a kind of vacuum occupied by nothing, the soundless milieu of a blank and all but mute existence. On the contrary it is a weighty silence; "a profound silence which is full of words", "lifegiving, refreshing, soothing, satisfying: a silence of substance" as Heller says.

But what does he mean? What is it that these words are trying to convey?

When speaking of a "profound silence which is full of words", he uses the phrase in the same sense as when one says that the colour white contains the colours of the whole spectrum. It is not then a vacuum, a negation, but a significant fullness. "His silence is the abdication of words before the Immense and the Unfathomable." He found himself with the mystery of a God made man, of a Virgin who conceived without the help of man, and of an election — by God of himself — to guard the mystery and protect those who shared it. What was he to say of such an event? He saw himself as a simple man, an artisan of a tiny town lost in a corner of the Empire. He was not only a spectator of the most marvellous event since the creation of the world, but a human being involved in it by God's special design. One does not speak when immersed in contemplating the divine. The grandeur of what one is contemplating is such that any word would appear trivial, for the event is well beyond the person involved in the contemplation, and far beyond anything he can say. In any case, it was not Joseph's responsibility to have something to say. His mission was different.

Nor was his silence that of a dreamer. As regards the imagination too, he was a silent man. For a man may not enunciate a single word and yet not be quiet within because of the torrent of images which disturb his soul and maintain it in an unreal world. Rather does Saint Joseph give the impression of being one who uses his imagination to serve his task, without the vain dreams of the weak-willed person or his confused stream of meaningless and aimless fantasies. Perhaps because he wasn't a dreamer, he was to be an effective person capable of carrying out his lofty undertaking, being more attentive to duty and to working hard than to imagining an unreal and fanciful distant future.

The Benefits of Silence

We first notice that Joseph's silence is not empty. It is a fully occupied silence. It has content. The first thing we can learn is that there is a silence which is beneficial, a silence which does not come from distraction or from the mind's being 'elsewhere', in 'another world', but from contemplation, which at the same time is a condition that makes interior growth possible. One cannot accommodate reflection, and even less contemplation, with verbosity. A minimum of silence is needed to concentrate on what we have before us, to resolve the questions which daily life frequently poses before our eyes. All this interior activity, which is a sign that man has supernatural life, requires a minimum of silence. It is like "the gatekeeper to the interior life" (*The Way,* no. 281).

Without it an interior life is impossible. Distraction, noise, the dazed condition provoked by a cacophony of simultaneous babbling, from disparate voices blaring at us from a thousand different directions, does not favour reflection. Nothing upsets the clear vision of the soul more than the turbulence stirred up by trivial preoccupations and by the swarm of banalities which demand our attention and make man shallow and inconsistent — something like the individuals in the colony of monkeys which Kipling describes in *The Adventures of Mowgli*.

A man who keeps quiet can listen, and a man who listens is able to learn much. Through his silence, Joseph was able to hear the angel reveal in his dream the great secret which was to affect not only his own life but that of all mankind. But it is very difficult to listen when one is incapable of containing the cataract of cliches and banal phrases that pour from a thousand lips. How is it possible to hear anything when one is bombarded by a deafening racket?

And there is also a silence implying fortitude in the silent one. Those who grumble about the contradictions that overtake them, about their ill luck; those who air their problems to the four winds; those who are always excusing themselves; those who are constantly explaining what they have done, why they have done it, what they have stopped doing, why they did not do it; those who, in the final analysis, need outside approval to feel moderately calm: these are men who have not learnt to shoulder responsibility. For to carry burdens without complaint and without letting the whole world know about them, to face personal problems without casting them on to other backs: this is to be responsible for one's own actions and decisions without sliding out of one's obligations with excuses and self-justification. If these point to anything, they indicate a lack of real character. This is what shows that a person has truly become a man. And there is great strength in the one who knows how to keep silent, in the one who directs the drive of his will and his attention to the situation in hand, to "the one thing necessary", instead of allowing his energies to be dissipated in a sterile and a more or less futile way over a thousand matters which are not his concern. It reminds us of the Athenians, those contemporaries of St Paul, of whom the Acts of the Apostles have to say that "they concerned themselves only with listening and narrating new things" (Acts 17:21). The words of Isaiah (30:15) could well be applied to Joseph: "in silentio et in spe erit fortitudo vestra", in quietness and in trust shall be your strength. For this silent man who hoped in God showed, in effect, his fortitude in difficult and compromising situations, bearing himself in a manner worthy of the confidence placed in him.

Some Consequences

It is always better to remain silent on what ought not to be spoken. It is pride or, at the least, a blind vanity, which gives us the impulse to say what would be better kept quiet. For at times we hurt others with our words. Or we turn them into missiles launched indiscriminately to hurt others on landing (if we do not, indeed, deliberately launch them with careful aim at the target where most damage will result). We think ourselves ingenious. It does not cause us undue concern to demonstrate our cleverness even at the cost of humiliating or ridiculing others. And we try to stand out over the others not so much by our own knowledge as by the expedient of taking our neighbour down a peg. A contemptuous word, a brief sarcastic phrase, is at times sufficient. Here resentment is born, here enmities, disputes, divisions; for "he who says what he ought not, hears what he does not like". And letting the tongue loose never brings any good. Some other words of Isaiah are not inappropriate to Joseph: "He did not cry out or lift up his voice or make it heard in the street" (Is 42:2). For he was not argumentative, nor did he spend his life complaining, excusing himself, nor did he argue stubbornly. He was neither rebellious, nor raucous, nor did he go through life relating his problems and worries ·to whomsoever would listen. Even less did he meddle in the affairs of others. He did not find the time to see defects in the conduct, in the way of life or in the behaviour of his neighbours.

We ought to be very careful about what we say. Words uttered today live on, perhaps for decades, in the minds of others. No one knows the consequences that may be unleashed, because once pronounced — or published — our words are beyond us and outside our control. They can drift from one person to another, day by day, month by month, perhaps for years, awakening profound echoes, plucking sensitive chords in other men which will lead them to work for good or to do evil. He who utters these words, writes them or publishes them, becomes partly responsible — whether he likes it or not — for all the good or evil consequences which will arise from them for years to come.

Joseph's silence, so full and dense, ought to make us think about the men of today. God knows, we speak too much. This man who could have related so many marvellous things, having been present for such a long time at the heart of a great mystery, keeps quiet. With his silence he protects the intimacy of what ought to remain hidden, shrouded as much from the idle and superficial curiosity of glances that flicker and shift restlessly from one thing to another, as from unbridled tongues whose one serious occupation seems to be to spread to the corners of the earth 'news', rumours and gossip which are important to nobody and harmful to all that hear.

In our epoch it seems unfortunate that the one mission, or the principal one, of the so called means of social communication ('the media') is to keep themselves continuously speaking or writing, on any and every topic. Such is the volume of noise, including that meaningless and not always muted 'background music' which is seen as a necessary substitute for silence, that it seems as if they wish to prevent at all costs the possibility of man's exercising his capacity for reflecting on matters of substance. Perhaps here lies the cause for our fellow men's having so little interior depth; the effort of being involved in a multiplicity of events of every kind which clamour for their attention from all sides has made them so superficial that confusion and interior poverty are the only fruits they can show for all this activity. Perhaps another of Heller's observations is also true: "Many who have nothing to say, speak, and beneath the noise of their words and the turbulence of their lives, they dissimulate the emptiness of their ideas and their feelings". Saint Joseph, on the other hand, who could talk of so many things, says nothing. He guards within himself the greatness he contemplates. And this is certainly what a man does to remain in peace, "lord of his soul and master of his silence".

Silence and reflection prevent simple external appearances, the surface of things and events, from being the opaque veil which obscures the essential reality of creation and of God's plan. Silence and reflection are like the eyes which penetrate those clouds which confuse objects and diffuse truths. Piercing through this cloudy cover allows us to reach what really matters, for it means silencing every kind of frenetic and discordant voice, enabling us to hear the live, clear and penetrating word of God speaking to men, to each one of us, through creatures and events. Thus Saint Joseph came to know the plan of God extremely well. And he could and did carry out, at any and every moment, what the Creator expected of him.

3

The Spouse of Mary

In a brief treatise on Saint Joseph at the end of *The Ascent of Mount Sion,* Bernardine of Laredo makes the following consideration: "There will be some points here that emerge naturally and directly from the text of the Gospel and which will thus be suitable for use in preaching. But some thoughts on these points will be more suitable for pondering through meditation than for being affirmed textually; these reflections are credible through the piety of faith. . . ."

Such propositions are more appropriate for meditation than for firm and categorical acceptance; they are credible, nonetheless, as Bernardine of Laredo says quite properly, with 'the piety of faith'. But this is not because there are no certainties, or at least no reliable conclusions, on which to base such beliefs. They are the kind of statements that indicate the manner in which Saint Joseph performed the mission to which he had been called and the circumstances in which he had to carry it out. It is from these pieces of information that we can either make confident deductions or establish certain consequences as being plausible, since they contradict nothing which is known to be certain, and since, as Bernardine himself says, "they are, in every respect, close to the doctrine of Truth". It is such utterances as these that are "more suitable for pondering through meditation"; and this is the criterion with which we can approach such special references to the person of Joseph as well as to some of the circumstances surrounding him.

When Joseph is mentioned for the first time in the Gospel, he is already a man linked with a woman: "and Jacob, the father of Joseph, the husband of Mary, of whom Jesus is born, who is called Christ" (Matt 1:17). In this brief text at the end of St Matthew's introduction to his Gospel, Joseph is seen as a descendant of David, as being of royal stock. St Luke, speaking of the census ordered by Cæsar Augustus, confirms this, saying: "Joseph, because he was of the house and lineage of David. . ." (Luke 2:4).

For quite some time — centuries — Joseph was thought of (and represented) as an old man. This was probably due to the influence of the *Protogospel of James* and other similar apocryphal documents. This particular *Protogospel,* which was in circulation and is mentioned in the third century, describes in a picturesque way how the priests of Jerusalem came to choose a spouse for our Lady. It assumes that she was confined to the temple from her infancy. When she was twelve, all the widowers of Judæa were convoked in the temple and given a test to see which of them had been elected by God to become engaged to Mary. Joseph, who turned up with the others, was selected because a dove apparently emerged from his staff and flew onto his head. On hearing the decision of the priests about his election, he excused himself saying "I am an old man; I have children. She, on the other hand, is young, and I fear the ridicule of the sons of Israel." The same approach to his age is seen in *The History of Joseph the Carpenter* (in the sixth or seventh century). Joseph is a "just old man", with four sons and two daughters, one of the twelve oldest men of the tribe of Juda convened by the priests. In some pious books he is called "the saintly old man Joseph".

Against this general opinion of Joseph's age is that of Bernardine of Laredo. And he well explains (or excuses) the erroneous opinion by pointing out that in the early Church there were heretics who claimed that Joseph was the natural father of Jesus. By way of refuting this heresy, paintings began to show "Saint Joseph as a man old in years". But to continue doing this after the heresy had been disposed of — he says — "was quite silly". And so it was. In the seventeenth century the argument was, with reasons which made good sense, in favour of Joseph's youth when he came to be engaged to Mary. It was obvious that Mary's honour would be better safeguarded by a young husband than by an old one and — as has been sensibly observed — the advanced age of an old man would make nonsense of the vow of chastity which, according to general opinion, Joseph had taken. And all of this does not take into account the circumstances that the Mother and Child were to encounter, which would have required the best efforts and the decisiveness of a young man. As with

Gerson, who saw him as a "young and comely", Fr Bernardine makes Joseph some forty years old, since "one concludes that a male begins his prime of life at the age of thirty-five, and remains in it until he is almost fifty".

A hundred years after Fr Bernardine, in the seventeenth century, a nun, Sister Maria de Jesus de Agreda, wrote about Saint Joseph and Our Lady in a very pious and devout way. Often what she has to say appears, perhaps, unduly picturesque; thus, for example, Mary sees the ten thousand angels who stand guard, and on occasion graciously commands them to do some small service. But in the midst of all this, she is perhaps closer to the truth and to Fr Bernardine in demonstrating Joseph's youth than was all the pictorial and literary tradition which assumed he was an old widower. The venerable Sister Maria attests, with great aplomb, that when they were engaged, Our Lady was fourteen and Joseph thirty-three, and that he was "of very noble character, courteous, pleasant and gentle".

These statements are nonetheless no more certain than are any of the others as regards the assumptions on which they are based. All are conjecture. However, since they accord with simple common sense, the opinions of Sister Maria de Jesus de Agreda appear to be more logical and closer to reality than the rest. The line of reasoning, that with an old man the perpetual virginity and refined purity of Our Lady is better explained than when having a young husband, appears to reveal a hidden lack of confidence in the capacity of youth to live a life of chastity. Mgr Escrivá, referring to this point not without a sense of humour, would exclaim "It is as if the condition for living holy purity is that one be old".

Why Jesus Was Born into a Family

That Jesus would be born in the midst of a family, even if it were such a small one as that of Joseph and Mary, was fully in consonance with God's plans. Both of them had their own role to play in the years which preceded the public life of the Redeemer; for each it would be a role which God himself had foreseen, one for which they had been selected and for whose accomplishment they had received supernatural instruction. St John Chrysostom (one of the Fathers who has written most extensively on Saint Joseph) points to four reasons for holding it convenient that this be so.

In the first place — he writes — so that the royal descent of the Virgin Mary would be patently clear, both St Matthew and St Luke make a special point that Saint Joseph was "of the house and family of David" as we have seen earlier. Thus it is clear that Mary too was of royal stock, since it was the inveterate custom of the Jews that marriage should take place between members of the same tribe. Maldonatus also affirms this in his *Commentaries*. There are other less solid and more forced arguments for Mary's being, like Joseph, of the tribe of Levi. It is deduced, for example, from her relationship with Elizabeth, the wife of Zachary.

In the second place, Chrysostom continues, Mary's honour would not have to suffer when she bore her child, nor would she incur punishment from the law. Evidently, to have conceived and given birth to a child without being married would have been equivalent to having incurred public disgrace. For although her virginity was to be preserved, and She, filled with grace, was to be the Mother of God, people would only see what was before their eyes.

And it would be difficult for a woman to avoid dishonour and defamation in a small town by having a child without a father. Jesus' position would not then be within the rules of the juridical order of his people and of his time. From the beginning he would have been, in a certain sense, discredited. The situation would have been even worse if one of the mandates of Deuteronomy were to be followed: "If the tokens of virginity are not found in the young woman, then they shall bring out the young woman to the door of her father's house, and the men of her city shall stone her to death, because she has wrought folly in Israel by playing the harlot in her father's house" (Deut 22:21).

The third reason is that an older man, however good and well disposed he ·might be, would be unlikely to have the energy and enterprise needed for the difficult and hurried flight into Egypt, there to begin a new life, with no assets but his own work, in the midst of a foreign people and in a land that favoured pagan customs. It would be rough. It would hardly bespeak a tranquil life.

He adds yet another reason — the fourth — taken, it seems, from St Ignatius of Antioch: it would be to conceal from the devil the birth of the Messiah. For when the angel Gabriel announced the mystery of the Incarnation to Mary, she was already engaged to Joseph. The betrothal was really the marriage, the "wedding" being only its perfection.

Why Mary Was Betrothed to Joseph

Centuries later, St Thomas Aquinas (S.Th. III q29 a1) would state twelve reasons why it was convenient for Our Lady to be united in matrimony to Joseph.

Some of these were his own and some were taken from Ambrose, Chrysostom and others. These include: to conceal His birth from the devil; so that Mary might not be stoned; that Jesus might not be taken for an illegitimate child; that someone might administer to them, etc. Our attention is also drawn to another reason which, as an argument for the virginity of Mary, St Thomas borrows from St Ambrose: "Her husband is the more trustworthy witness of her purity, in that he would deplore the dishonour and avenge the disgrace were it not that he acknowledged the mystery".

Leaving aside the greater or lesser persuasive power of each one of the reasons of convenience to which St John Chrysostom and St Thomas refer, one has, above all, to consider the obvious reason — that of common sense. And because this is the case, it cannot be stated explicitly enough. Every child needs a family. And there is no proper family — it is incomplete — if there is only a woman, although she may be the Blessed Virgin Mary. A home needs not only a large heart — and it is the woman who always provides this in the home — but also a head. God could obviously have done without Joseph. He did not need him at all for the Virgin Mary to conceive the Saviour. But within this context he could also have prescinded from Mary. The Omnipotent God could have chosen a thousand other ways to carry out the Redemption.

But this particular plan is the one decreed by divine providence. In it the Only Begotten Word of the Father had to become man, taking flesh in the most pure womb of Our Lady. He would be born in the midst of a family, in harmony with the people, the place and the time of his coming into the world.

It seems that this plan was to be carried out without major unusual interventions. It is a fact that miracles are not squandered to supply what can be obtained — and should be — in a natural way by common or garden means. Both the Mother and her Son needed someone to fulfil the role of head of the family, not only to earn a living for them, but also, as far as others were concerned, in social relations and in the education of the child.

In brief, the scandalous situation of a single woman who is the mother of a child did not figure in God's plans. St Ambrose writes that Our Lord preferred his origin to be doubted (and that people should take him for the son of Joseph) rather than to have the purity of his mother questioned. St John of Avila says that Our Lord "did not want the lips of men to speak of her having a son without a husband. He preferred that they esteem him the son of an unworthy man, (being as he was the son of the Eternal Father), rather than to doubt the good name of his sacred mother". But she was not either to be a woman married to a man and to give him other children. Jesus, the Son of God, ought to be born in a family belonging to the chosen people, for he had to fulfil the prophecies (son of Abraham, son of David). Legally, he ought to have not only a mother but also a father. Thus the Virgin Mary should be married, and, for the second condition to be fulfilled, the man to be her spouse would love her and be sufficiently a man to respect her virginal purity. Joseph was just the man whom Jesus chose to play this difficult part. And "all Joseph's sanctity lies in the most scrupulous fulfilment of his mission, which is so great and so humble, so high and so hidden, so splendid and so mysteriously shrouded" (Pius XI).

A True Marriage

Today hardly anyone feels that the word 'espoused' is merely equivalent to our word 'engaged'. But Maldonatus had sought many witnesses to refute this opinion. When Scripture refers to Our Lady as the *spouse* of Joseph ("Joseph, fili David, ne timeas accipere Mariam *conjugem*" Matt 1:10) it shows that they were betrothed, not merely engaged. And although "it is not a loss of virginity but a testimony of marriage that they declare solemn nuptials", we nevertheless guard against thinking that the marriage of Joseph and Mary was only a legal fiction. They married because they loved one another. And it was when they were espoused — without having as yet celebrated the wedding — that God revealed his plans for them, first to the Virgin Mary, and then to Joseph. It was a true marriage. Both pledged to each other the reciprocal rights over their bodies as regards generation; both voluntarily and freely, with full knowledge of their responsibility, renounced the exercise of their rights. For as St Augustine argues against Julian, the essence of matrimony does not consist in its use. "Should it happen" — he writes in *De Nuptiis et Concupiscentiis* — "that by mutual consent they agree to abstain forever from the use of carnal concupiscence, this does not break the conjugal tie. On the contrary, it is stronger when the promises made are more carefully and mutually observed, than with the sensual bond. Not in vain, then, did the angel say to Joseph: 'Do not fear to take Mary as your spouse.' In this way Mary is called *spouse* by reason of her commitment, although her spouse had not come close to her nor was he to do so later".

Joseph loved Our Lady, not with a brotherly love but with a pure conjugal love. It was so deep that any carnal relation was made totally superfluous. So refined was it that he became not only a witness of Mary's virginal purity — virgin before birth, in birth and after birth as the Church teaches — but he became its custodian. . . Nor was it necessary for Joseph to be of an advanced age to live in complete chastity with his wife. His very love for the most marvellous creature who has ever existed was sufficient guarantee. "Joseph had a young heart and a young body when he married Mary, when he learned of the mystery of her divine motherhood, when he lived in her company, respecting the integrity God wished to give the world as one more sign that he had come to share the life of his creatures" writes Mgr Escrivá. "Anyone who cannot understand a love like that knows very little of true love, and is a complete stranger to the christian meaning of chastity." And such a person would find it even more difficult than it otherwise might be to approach anywhere near the love Mary and Joseph had for each other.

With such a powerful manifestation of the supernatural (and both had experienced it) even nature itself becomes appeased and 'forgets' an impulse which exists, in any event, only in the species of man and not in the individual. "Sufficit tibi gratia", My grace is enough. St Paul had heard this from the lips of our Lord (II Cor 12:9). How much more is it so in this case, when grace abounds? It abounds in that humble man, who agonised so grievously before the angel was to communicate to him the reason for his marriage to Mary.

4

Being A Just Man . . .

The snatches of information on Saint Joseph which have reached us are centred on a dilemma. In that first scene of the Gospel it is already possible to glimpse something of Joseph's qualities and of the difficulty of the mission entrusted to him. Joseph was betrothed to Mary, and "before they came together she was found to be with child" (Matt 1:18). They were already husband and wife, because the betrothal ceremony had the full force of matrimony. However, they had not yet celebrated the wedding. This consists in the solemn conducting of the bride to the home of the bridegroom to begin their life together. According to Jewish custom, since women were very young when they were given in matrimony, they used to live in their parents' home for a period of time — normally a year — before moving to their new home.

Although St Luke does not mention Joseph when he is dealing with Our Lady's visitation to St Elizabeth, this silence does not necessarily mean that he was absent. Those authors who come down in favour of Joseph's being present in the little village in the mountains of Judæa where Elizabeth and Zachary lived are by no means on the wrong track. Bearing in mind that they were betrothed, and recalling how young Mary was, it is far from fanciful (indeed, it is well nigh common sense) to assert that her husband, Joseph, would have accompanied her on her outward journey. And he would also have gone to fetch her when, after the birth of John the Baptist had taken place, Mary returned once again to Nazareth. What is not so easy to maintain is his presence when Mary greeted Elizabeth, and the latter, filled with the Holy Spirit, revealed the mystery. For on this assumption Joseph's later doubts and perplexities could not really be understood. But neither is this an adequate argument to the contrary, because although Elizabeth's words were enough to arouse suspicion that something out of the ordinary was taking place, they nevertheless did not reveal Mary's virginal conception. Of course, what is not likely, and may even perhaps be quite implausible, is to have Joseph not only Mary's companion on the journey but also a guest of Zachary throughout the time she was there, as some ancient authors have surmised.

Sister Maria of Agreda is among those who like to contemplate Joseph keeping Mary company on this by no means short journey. The refined (and sometimes penetrating) observations which her devotion leads her to make are quite remarkable. Commenting on Our Lady's return from Elizabeth's home, accompanied by Joseph, she reckoned that Our Lady was conscious of the fact that it would be impossible to conceal her condition for much longer. And she adds "with these thoughts in her mind, she gazed at him now with greater tenderness and compassion because of the shock which was about to befall him. And she would have wished to spare him this if it were God's will. But the Lord did not respond to this concern of hers because he had arranged the event with means which were appropriate for His glory and meritorious both for Joseph and for His Virgin Mother".

Joseph's Reaction to Mary's Conception

In fact, it was in Nazareth and after those months during which Mary was keeping St Elizabeth company that Joseph saw that his wife was pregnant. That fact must have been a heavy blow for him, a bitter surprise which was completely out of keeping with the opinion he held of Mary, but a fact for which it was scarcely possible for him to seek anything but a natural cause. It was difficult enough to believe it. But be that as it may, he had to believe it because the reality stared him in the face. Like a nightmare which might vanish as quickly as a bad dream might pass away, the fact must have weighed on his spirit like a stone slab. It seemed an impossibility that Mary, his betrothed, could have done anything that might be wrong. And yet the days passed. This was no bad dream, no nightmare. There was no explanation, only a reality which he had to accept because what is real always ends by imposing its authority.

How indeed could he think that Mary had offended God? For him this was simply inconceivable. Yet "reasoning could not belie what was obvious to the eyes. Sometimes he dismissed his suspicions", continues Sister Maria of Agreda, "and at other times the evidence made them grow." In this state of uncertainty time went by, without his knowing what decision to take.

The cause of the conflict which made St Joseph suffer so much for a time has not always been seen in this way. The evangelist says that "before they came together she was found to be with child by the power of the Holy Spirit" (Matt 1:18). Such an event was unimaginable for Joseph, something truly bewildering, especially bearing in mind Mary's intention — which he knew about and with which he was identified — of maintaining her virginal consecration to God. What ought he to do? He pondered on it and reached a conclusion. "Joseph, her husband, being a just man, did not wish to have her put to shame, and resolved to send her away quietly" (Matt 1:19).

The Fathers of the Church

The Fathers and commentators agree in recognising Joseph's *justice* which is both logical and natural, given what the evangelist says. But where or in what way did his justice show itself? Why was it emphasised that he was a *just* man precisely when he decides to forsake his wife secretly? Why does the quality of being a just man show itself precisely in this decision?

On this point there is no commonly held explanation. Some of the Fathers, like St John Chrysostom, St Augustine and St Ambrose, with the freedom given them by the simplicity with which they sought spiritual progress through the literal comprehension of the sacred text, concentrate on Joseph's holiness. They assume him to hold the obvious explanation of

Mary's condition and that he bore the terrible trial without being dragged down by any natural reaction. With that apparent lack of inhibition with which they sometimes used to express themselves, and which at times sounds somewhat crude to our sensibilities, St Augustine wrote: "He knew, indeed, that she was not bearing his child and therefore took her for an adulteress . . . . As a husband he was very upset. But as a just man he shows himself not to be cruel. This man's holiness was so great that he neither wished to keep an adulteress with him, nor did he presume to punish her by making public her dishonour . . .".

St John Chrysostom, for his part, agrees substantially with St Augustine, although he puts it with greater precision. "But Joseph not only took into account the greater misfortune of the punishment of death, but also the lesser — that of the Virgin Mary's shame. He not only did not wish to punish her; he did not intend submitting her to public dishonour either . . . . Joseph was so free from passion that he did not wish Our Lady to be hurt in any way whatsoever. To keep her in his home seemed to be against the law. To get rid of her and take her to the courts was to send her to certain death. Joseph does neither of these things. Rather his behaviour rises above the law."

Modern Explanations

Today there are few, if any, who go along with this explanation. It is incompatible with a very important fact, one which it seems was overlooked at that time. Perhaps this was because the consequences which follow from the exceptional and unique status of the Virgin Mary had scarcely been developed. And so a more profound insight has

become apparent. Another more accurate explanation — less natural and more supernatural — has
gained acceptance nowadays. This explanation is
thus more in harmony with what Our Lady was and
with Saint Joseph's holiness. Fr Francisco Suarez,
echoing this development in one of his *Disputæ,*
quotes as one of its most important manifestations
the text of the *Auctor imperfecti,* which deserves to
be widely known: "Oh how incomparable is this
praise of Mary! Saint Joseph believed rather in
the chastity of his betrothed than in what his eyes
saw, in grace rather than in nature. He saw plainly
that his betrothed was a mother but he could not
believe that she was an adulteress. He believed that
it was more possible for a woman to conceive without
a man than for Mary to commit a sin."

Of course, Joseph did not know what had taken
place. Some recent explanations are so far-fetched as
to assert that Joseph knew what had happened;
and that this was made known to him by Our Lady,
not directly but through her mother St Anne. It is
obvious that if he had been aware of the mystery not
only would the revelation conveyed to him in dreams
have been quite superfluous, but in addition, all
Joseph's uncertainty, which shines through the text
of the gospel, as to what he ought to do, loses its
burden of anguish. And although the devout Fr
Bernardine of Laredo wrote that the Angel's revelation to Joseph was not to enlighten him about what
he already knew "and held for a certainty, through
the admirable radiance of her angelic countenance
and the perfect sanctity which he recognised in the
most holy Virgin", it is still not possible to accept
readily "the divine brilliance which only he merited
to see in the Virgin's countenance from the first
moment that she became pregnant by the power of

God." As in the apocryphal writings there are, at times, assertions in some devout authors which are useless as a basis for a better comprehension of the text, because there is no evidence for them except in their imagination or devotion.

The authors of the notes to the Jerusalem Bible pose the question in this way. "The justice of Joseph undoubtedly consists in his not wishing to conceal with his name a child whose father he did not know. But being convinced of Mary's virtue, neither does he refer to the rigorous process of the law (Deut 22:20 *et seq*) this mystery which he does not understand." For its part, Spadafora's Dictionary says: "As he was a just man, while not harbouring the slightest suspicion against his wife's integrity, he wished in the face of the incomprehensible to conceal the mystery and to eclipse himself personally."

Joseph's Solution

Joseph's state of perplexity had its origin, then, in the contradiction between the two events, or facts, which were certain and firmly established in his mind. On the one hand was the certain fact that Our Lady was going to be a mother without his intervention, and on the other, his conviction not only of the purity of his spouse but also of her sanctity. This being so it was blatantly unjust to denounce her. For the punishment established in Deuteronomy — stoning — would have been imposed on her. And he was a just man. Such a solution was ruled out from the beginning. Give her perhaps a writ of dismissal? This was, of course, within the legal provisions established among the Jews. By means of this document both parties recovered their freedom and were enabled to restart their lives. But Our Lady was similarly dishonoured by this solution because a man who disavowed his pregnant wife before they came to live together was proclaiming to the world that there had been some guilt there. In future, Mary would always be a woman whose husband had dismissed her publicly and legally — and, moreover, even before receiving her into his home! It is not difficult to realise the significance of this in a small village where everyone knew each other and where subjects of conversation were neither plentiful nor very wide-ranging. What could have happened? What could she have done that her husband should have sent her away from him in such a forthright and abrupt manner, so soon after they were betrothed? To take this step amounted to turning Our Lady into a branded woman.

The other solution which Joseph thought of adopting would also have got around this problem, but its results would have been really very different. To put her away privately meant simply avoiding the issue, leaving unfulfilled the marriage to which he had solemnly committed himself with the betrothal ceremony. In this case and with this solution Our Lady would not now be a rejected wife but an abandoned wife. Not a woman marked out by sin but one marked by misfortune. Not a woman expiating a misdeed, but one who suffers for someone else's misdeed. Moreover, with this solution there was a guilty party only to the extent that he appeared to be one — the sort of man who does not keep his word and deserts his wife and the child of their marriage without any explanation.

Joseph was a just man, the gospel tells us. And being just, of all the decisions that were open to him he took that one with regard to Our Lady which least harmed her although it was not exactly the most suitable for himself.

In deciding "to put her away secretly", he demonstrated that he was a just man, that is to say, a saint. Thus although we do not know what kind of impulse led him to reject repudiation, recovering his own freedom and granting the same to his wife, the fact is that it seems as if he might have had an intuition of the indissolubility of marriage — in spite of Jewish law. Certainly the solution he adopted amounted to acknowledging that a commitment freely undertaken before witnesses united him for life to the woman he had taken for his wife. His justice — not for nothing was he *vir justus,* a just man — led him to abide by the consequences of a decision which did not only concern himself. No, he had no truck with a legal abuse which Moses had authorised because of the hardness of heart of the Jews. He did not have a hard heart and so he adhered to God's law. He refused to take refuge in man-made legality even though God tolerated it. He would not receive his wife but he would remain united to her because he stood by his pledged word. St John of Avila summed up Joseph's decision in this soliloquy: "The most suitable measure and one which is as well for me to adopt in such a doubtful case, is to leave her and go away secretly, so that nobody can ask me why. So I shall neither discredit her nor put myself in danger by living with her if she is not good. Nor dare I be with her if she is so holy that God has worked in her the miracle of having conceived without me or any other man."

Perhaps it was Riccioti who, following St Jerome, sums up the question in a more logical and fitting manner. "In a case of this kind, an upright and honourable Jew, once convinced of the guilt of his wife, would have divorced her without further ado. He would consider himself not only to be in the right, but perhaps under an obligation to proceed in this way, since a silent and passive toleration could seem like consent and complicity. But Joseph, precisely because he was *a just man,* did not behave like this. Moreover, he was convinced of Mary's innocence and therefore deemed it wicked to submit her to the dishonour of a public divorce."

What is True Justice?

The word 'just' suggests to everyone the idea of justice. A just man is one who acts with justice. If he did not act thus, he would not be just, but unjust. In coming to his decision, to the precise one which got over the problem without harming Our Lady, or with the least possible harm, Joseph acted with justice. What is more important is that he showed he was a just man. For an unjust man can sometimes act with justice without, in doing so, losing his tendency to be unjust in the same way as a liar can sometimes tell the truth without ceasing to be a liar. It is very difficult, if not impossible, to act unjustly always, or always to tell lies about everything.

It is, then, each one's quality of being just which matters much more than any other thing, and even more than an isolated action which in itself may not be significant. The one who possesses the quality of being just is the one who regularly behaves with justice. But what is it to behave with justice?

Justice is a word which, like some others (freedom, democracy, rights, etc.) is heard of a great deal in the western world but which nevertheless (like the others) has a content assigned to it which usually detracts from or falsifies the true meaning of the word. Hence we have to be careful in the use of words, so as not to cause harm, giving to understand one thing instead of another, and creating mental confusion which then hinders upright behaviour.

The true function of justice is to give to each person what is his due. If we want to be just, we have, of course, to be prepared to give each one what belongs to him. But this must be *without excluding God* since it seems as if we habitually think only of our fellow man when we speak of justice. What is it, then, to be just towards God? Clearly to give him what is his, what belongs to him. And what is it that belongs to God, that is his, that we have to give him in order to behave with justice?

In a word, everything. St Paul puts this in terms as clear as they are accurate. "What do you have that you have not received?" (I Cor 4:7). And on another occasion: "We belong to God" (Rom 14:8). Indeed it is from Him that we have received our senses and our intelligence, goods both material and spiritual, and the thousand and one things of creation. But there is something still more important. From him we have received our being and existence, and not only in the natural sphere but in the supernatural as well.

Who is a Just Man?

Thus, a just man, is fundamentally, a committed man. He is a man who acknowledges that he has received everything, and that in consequence he is indebted for everything, a man who considers that he is under obligation to give back to God honour, glory, praise, adoration and gratitude for all that he has received. Such a man knows that he will not find a better way of fulfilling this duty of justice, to which every man is bound to devote himself so that God may work as He wishes in him and with him. In a word, to be just is to be holy. Thus, Joseph would choose the solution most beneficial to Our Lady, the one which would cause her least harm.

Perhaps, then, one must come to the conclusion that justice (but not any kind of justice, not merely legal or human justice but justice according to God) includes among its properties a certain vein of compassion, of mercy, which prevents or minimizes the harm done to others. Joseph did not simply stop at *his* right but at something which, from a higher standpoint, went beyond it. To behave with justice towards God entails holiness, that is, love: love of God and love of neighbour for God's sake. And so it is that kind of justice to which Jesus referred when he told us that if someone should steal our cloak we should give him our tunic too (instead of going to the police or assaulting the thief). And if someone should compel us to journey a mile with him, we should gladly journey two miles more (Matt 5:40-41). The justice of a just man amply demonstrates this in the situation we are considering in that Joseph thought more about the honour of Mary than about his own. He is in conformity with the gospel's teaching us to return good for evil and to bless the one who curses us (Luke 6:28). And therefore he is already on that higher plane to which Jesus referred when he said that he had come not to destroy the law, but to bring it to perfection, to give to it its complete fulfilment (Matt 5:17). On the other hand, and in a similar situation to this one, who can presume to hold in his hand *all* the elements of a wise judgement?

The greatness or meanness of a man is shown by the generous or selfish way he looks at things. Or better still, by the generous or selfish way in which he behaves. And a man's qualities are put to the test above all at those times when what is being weighed in the balance is what he carries within himself. Joseph, seemingly a man of no importance, showed a greatness of spirit which one rarely encounters. But one has to detect men of this calibre, because, like precious metals, they are usually hidden. Very often they themselves are unaware of their own greatness.

It is the difficult situations which demonstrate what a man is like inside, what he really is. That kind of situation forces a man to show on the surface that best or worst of himself which dwells in the depths of his soul. And Joseph, thrust into the heart of the problem, brought the best out of himself. Being a man of the highest moral fibre, he showed what he had in abundance.

5

While He Reflected . . .

Joseph's decision to forsake Mary unobtrusively was not taken on the spur of the moment. It was not a reaction provoked by consideration of the event itself. Nor was it the instantaneous reply to a provocation, the kind of instinctive reflex action one produces before one has even had time to grasp the nature of the problem. Neither was his decision swayed by wounded pride or damaged self-respect, nor was it influenced by any of the other many self-interested responses which similar experiences can arouse in men. Important issues need unhurried and thoughtful attention, although not everyone may realise this or be capable of it. In this case the matter was vitally important not only for Joseph but for Mary too. And Joseph was sufficiently mature to grant the dilemma the attention it merited. He would not deal with it lightly.

What was at stake was not honour alone, but also love. Mary's honour was safeguarded with the decision he had adopted. Once the preservation of her good name was resolved upon, his own reputation, which was scarcely of equal importance to him, would remain practically intact, although perhaps a little dented. But it was the second aspect which was especially distressing. Joseph loved Mary, and here lay the roots of the seriousness of his quandary. For when the heart and the head are pulling in opposite directions heartbreak becomes inevitable. The heart of a man in love tends with an almost irresistible force towards the woman he loves. But if his head tells him he must fight that impulse, the result is suffering.

In Joseph's case the dilemma was even more acute because it must have seemed to him almost impossible to come to a decision. Rather than easing or lessening its seriousness, the passage of time made the finding of a solution ever more urgent, although the situation became no clearer no matter how much he reflected on it. It was like a cul-de-sac, with no way out. To all appearances Mary was guilty. But he was convinced that this simply could not be so; he was certain of her innocence.

The contrast between what he saw with his own eyes and what he knew of his spouse cannot but have increased his bewilderment and indecision. Mary's silence did not help. Why did she not speak? Why did she not say *anything?* Wasn't *some* explanation, weren't a few words, due to him? She certainly did not act like a guilty woman. She showed no shame as one might expect in a girl whose offence is now evident. Her eyes showed no embarrassment. Her looks were as pure, as noble and serene as ever. At times she even looked at him with compassion. In

appearance she was not downcast; she must sometimes even have seemed radiant. Her behaviour was
not that of one who is under severe pressure because
of the trauma of having to explain what is visible and
yet not being able to admit the obvious. She gazed at
him; she suffered because he was suffering . . . but
she maintained her silence. From where did she get
the strength, that inner support, which would allow
her in such a tense situation to carry on living her
normal daily life just as always, without going to
pieces?

It is impossible to know how long this period of
puzzled anguish and conflicting emotions lasted.
(Sister Maria de Agreda airily says it was two months
and she may well have been right.) Taking into
account Mary's condition, her incomprehensible silence and bafflingly serene attitude, it is more than
possible that Joseph took quite some time before
deciding what to do. But *haec autem eo cogitante*
(Matt 1:20), as he considered this solution, which he
had arrived at, examining it from different points of
view, trying to see if it really was an adequate resolu-
tion of the problem, a revelation came to him. This
would be after he had passed days and nights in
agonised and obsessive reflection, without being able
to confide in anyone, or to catch even one clear
glimpse of the way ahead. Now, at last, his mind
made up, he could find some respite. And then,
while he rested, the real solution came to him, a
solution startlingly and altogether different from the
one he had just chosen. With it came flooding in
peace and joy. "Behold, an angel of the Lord appeared to him in a dream saying 'Joseph, son of
David, do not fear to take Mary as your wife, for that
which is conceived in her is of the Holy Spirit' " (Matt
1:20-23).

Joseph, it seems, hesitated about receiving Mary as his wife. They were betrothed, but as the wedding (or second and concluding part of the marriage) had not yet been celebrated, she had still to be conducted to the house of her spouse. The quandary having arisen, it would be difficult to avoid repercussions on this final stage of their union. In view of the unforeseen and unimaginable new factors which had arisen, Joseph would naturally be hesitant about taking this further step. It was certainly through no remaining fear of dishonour, for if the worst came to the worst, marriage would have kept the secret. It was fear, perhaps, of managing things badly before God by desecrating a mystery of which he now had a foreboding.

We will never know. Nor does it matter. The fact is that whatever was the cause of his fear of receiving Mary into his home and of celebrating the marriage, the fear disappeared as soon as the angel made him party to this great mystery. This enlightenment as to God's designs for man definitively (as it were) introduced him to the work of the Redemption. In the words of Edith Stein, "this Redemption had been conceived and accomplished in the abyss of mysterious depths, in silence and in secret". It was in silence and in secret that the annunciation of the mystery was made to Our Lady, and silently and secretly the Incarnation of the Son of God took place. In silence and in secret Joseph was purified in those agonising days of trial. And in the same silence and secrecy Joseph, son of David, received the news which he had to know. For he could not accomplish the mission which God had decided was his, without knowing at least those essential elements of it which were to affect him. The angel calmed his fears and revealed to him the stupendous mystery of the

Incarnation. Thus he learned of the service he was to perform. As soon as he became aware of it he responded, acting with the same promptitude and totally unconditional submission with which Mary, his spouse, had responded a few months earlier to the divine plan which the angel had conveyed to her.

Real Solutions Follow from Reflection

Exsurgens de somno, waking from his sleep, St Matthew continues, "he did as the angel of the Lord had commanded him and took to himself his wife" (Matt 1:24). "Waking from his sleep . . . ", as one coming out of a nightmare, emerging from a situation so strange that it seems unreal, and as anomalous as those absurd and monstrous ravings which fever provokes in the delirious. Or perhaps on being freed after the angel's revelation from doubt and indecision, and consequently resolving to receive his spouse, he was leaving a world of darkness and confusion to enter into the light which unequivocally showed the sure road he had to follow.

The circumstances in which the mystery is revealed to him, precisely when he is reflecting on these things, is not without significance. God could clearly have spared him suffering by acquainting him with the divine plan at the same time, for example, as he revealed it to the Virgin Mary. She too would then have been spared the anguish of seeing Joseph suffer and of herself having to keep a secret which otherwise would immediately have resolved his problem. God does not pay attention to the way men see things. He lets Our Lady suffer. For some time he permits Joseph to debate in anguished confusion, understanding nothing, and seeing no clear way out, not knowing exactly what he ought to do in a situation as unforeseeable as it was delicate and painful. It was only when he arrived at an honourable solution consonant with his (imperfect) knowledge of reality that God intervened by means of his angel. The true solution reached Joseph as soon as he had done all he could in his circumstances, without omitting anything that depended on him or was within his power. Only then, not earlier, did God let him know what was necessary for him in order to rectify his erroneous decision. And with this as a point of reference, as St John Chrysostom says, "the angel directs Joseph to the prophet Isaiah so that, on awakening, he will not forget what only recently he has learnt. Furthermore, as he had been nurtured on these same prophetic passages, he will recall them constantly and through them he will remember the exact words".

Seeking the Advice of Others

The degree of affliction Joseph had to suffer is not so common as to be within the experience of most men. But in a different way we all have to pass through critical phases which perhaps have some similarity with Joseph's experience. Whether they be called dilemmas, thorny problems or enormous obstacles somehow to be surmounted, there are in the lives of nearly all men difficult moments which do not concern themselves alone. These are moments in which one is forced to make a choice which can irreversibly change the course of one's life and that of others. Those who have not undergone this kind of suffering cannot easily understand it. At such times only a special attitude will lead to justice in the solution adopted. When heart and reason are at loggerheads, and we feel torn apart internally, when the heart beats faster, it is then, and especially then, that it is important to avoid making a decision. This is the moment to check oneself, to reflect, so that one is not submerged in a welter of emotion. For just as the heart has been made to love, the head is there to think and to show the heart which course to follow.

What Joseph teaches here is that when faced with a difficult problem, a cruel dilemma or an apparently immovable obstacle (and it is a fact of life that not one of us is exempt from these), the first action proper to man is reflection. Just solutions are not achieved on impulse, on a hunch, or on an instinctive or precipitate reaction. The only result of such a decision is to complicate the situation further, adding new difficulties or aggravating the problem. To hope it will resolve itself or that others will solve it for us is not the correct course. For there are times when no one else can make such decisions for us. One has to be sufficiently mature to take them oneself and face the consequences. There are men who will never grow up, locked as they are in an immaturity from which they don't seem to want to escape. When such men are in difficulty they invariably have recourse to others — not to seek advice (which is a prudent measure and much wiser than guessing or tossing a coin) but to throw their own responsibilities onto the shoulders of somebody else.

Recourse to others should only come about after seeing if one is able, unaided, to extricate oneself from the difficult situation and find an adequate solution. If the affair is such that it can be conveniently communicated, it is never too difficult to seek the opinion or advice of someone who can elucidate the problem for us or help us to a better solution. At the same time, to stick to one's own view in the face of more informed opinion is a sign of immaturity and stubbornness. It is as if to clutch an error to oneself were a proof of personality, or that all the rest of the world were wrong. Not even Joseph, in the end, emerged from the dilemma on his own; he did so with the help of the angel and by following his advice.

Those who have to be self-sufficient (because, given the nature of their problem, they cannot go to anyone else) are in Joseph's shoes. They cannot dispense with reflection. Reflection, not doubts. For there are some who feel that doubting is an activity (or even a method!) which is not only legitimate but thoroughly adequate. Perhaps they believe that by maintaining a sceptical frame of mind towards anything involving the world of the supernatural, their position will be that of a thinking person. In reality, it is precisely then that they are not in any such position.

He reflects who *really* wants to find a solution or longs to do what he ought. One cannot be fair towards anybody when proceeding without reflection. Thoughtlessness blinds and over-enthusiasm prevents any consideration of those factors or circumstances which should not be ignored. Those who trust so blindly to their intuition that they allow themselves the luxury of not thinking things over are those who commit the gravest errors with the greatest frequency. Often it is they who embarrass and harm others by their petulance and impatience. It is not so much through deliberate evil but through a shallow approach, a lack of depth, that harm and sorrow are caused to innocent people; these become the victims of superficiality and of misplaced self-confidence. When a problem or a blurred, difficult or delicate situation arises, reflection is the path to be adopted in the search for a proper and just solution. For reflection is none other than pondering on the facts, the factors and the circumstances of the question, inter-relating them with a view to finding out what course is required of us and what the reply is to be. Neither shallowness in judgement nor a surface substitute for thinking is the best road to success: they are in fact the worst. Perhaps it is for this reason that so many of our contemporaries commit so many and such grave errors by not adequately and conscientiously considering the information, the facts and the factors before they act. Thinking them to be too insignificant, what our modern man is doing is scorning the profound realities — which, too, are facts and solid ones.

It was reflection which disposed Joseph for the reception of the divine message. But it was not simple reflection on its own that brought him to discover what was beyond all human capacity to comprehend. Nor was it Our Lady who rid him of his doubts: her attitude could have been one of the reasons why he found it so difficult to come to a conclusion. Humanly speaking, her silence was an enigma for him. Why did not Our Lady give him any explanation, seeing him suffering as he was? Perhaps Joseph asked her and She could only confess her innocence. For the origin of her condition was a secret which did not belong to her. In any case, what is certain is that God only intervened through an angel when Joseph had done everything he could.

Further Preparation

Two further attendant circumstances are noteworthy here and have a lesson for us. As regards the first and more immediate one — the knowledge given

him of the mystery of the Incarnation of the Word —
to receive it, Joseph would need to have recovered a
minimum of peace and calm. Without this he would
not have been able to grasp the angel's message. It is
well known that a perturbed and troubled mind is
not in the best condition to recognise the supernatural; nor is a mind in such a state able to reason
clearly on purely human matters. For the second —
the mystery of God's plan for redeeming man in
which Joseph had been allocated a task — it was
perhaps the suffering and the purification this suffering had brought about in him, which prepared him
for the knowledge, understanding and significance of
what was to be revealed to him. Joseph was not filled
with grace as Our Lady was. He needed preparation.
With suffering comes purification (when one re-
sponds to it in the right way) and purification gives
man the capacity to perceive God's designs, his
omniscient plans for us. Such purification eliminates
the mental flux of fantasy, the superfluous train of
trivia which prevents one from thinking deeply about
the serious matter in hand.

The answer to the dilemma was revealed to Joseph
haec autem eo cogitante, while he was considering
this. What one cannot expect is light from God when
all the resources a man has at his disposal have not
been used to arrive at a just solution. When problems affect other people (not merely things, business
or any other purely external affairs) knowing what
reality is is important. Unfortunately, most men do
not come to discover who they themselves are. They
are so busy looking outside and round about them
that they end by ignoring completely what they carry
within. Such men hide themselves within the press of
people surrounding them. They adopt their conven-
tions, their way of thinking, their changing fashions,

their 'life-style'. They are like liquids with no consistency, conforming themselves to the shape of any mould because they lack any form of their own. On facing a difficulty, instead of inquiring what it is that God wants of them, and then seeking a proper solution accordingly, they look to the prevailing criteria and to the values of the society in which they are submerged. This way man attracts to himself a bewildering variety of evils of very different colours.

The answer — illumination from on high — came to Joseph in the same lonely condition as he was in when he was previously grappling with the problem. It came to him in a simple, unobtrusive and silent way, accompanied by nothing externally appreciable to the senses. It came from outside and beyond himself. It showed him that his own solution, although just, was not the one. And Joseph rectified his decision immediately, retracted his solution and immediately began working in harmony with what the angel had revealed. But one must bear in mind a detail which Mgr Escrivá noticed. "He never avoided reflecting on events, and so," — he continues — "was able to reach that level of understanding of the works of God which is wisdom."

6

He Took His Wife To His Home

The message the angel communicated to Joseph in his dream led him to a complete change of attitude. At first he was afraid to receive Mary; then he deliberated over leaving her unobtrusively. Finally, having learned from the angel's revelation what had happened, once awakened from his dream "he did as the angel had commanded him: he took his wife to his home" (Matt 1:24).

Here the expression "he took his wife" refers to the wedding. Mary and Joseph were betrothed. "Before they came to live together", before the solemn and festive procession of the wife to the house of the husband, Joseph had begun to have his doubts and fears. Thus the wedding itself was celebrated after Joseph learned of his own vocation, and of the role which God expected he would play in the lives of the Child and its Mother.

With the Virgin's reception into his home, Joseph assumed consciously and fully, with all the consequences that his decision would entail in the future, everything that God had shown him to be the purpose of his life. Just as the *fiat* pronounced by Our Lady implied a total and absolute dedication, including her renunciation of the right to lead her own life, (for in future she would be at the service of the Son to whom she would give birth), so too did Joseph accept his dedication to God by receiving Mary into his home. It was as if God himself had sealed their union in a definitive way. The angel had said "do not fear to take *Mary, your spouse* . . .". Now God was adding another even stronger bond than the betrothal. It was to be their common destiny on earth to look after, protect and help the as yet unborn Saviour. Both now shared the tremendous secret. And they — with Elizabeth in a different way — were the only ones in the whole world to know.

He took her to his home but "knew her not until she had borne a son." This does not mean to say that later on he *would* know her in the sense of having conjugal relations. The preposition 'until' does not necessarily imply a fixed period of time as the limit of an action or of an omission. In fact, as has been observed of old, the word appears in Scripture with several distinct meanings. At times it merely indicates a term, without in any way indicating what happens after that. St Jerome — as St Thomas Aquinas recalls — quotes a verse in Psalm 122: "Our eyes are raised to the Lord *until* he has mercy on us," pointing out that this does not mean that they turn away from God as soon as He shows mercy. In the second book of Samuel (6:23) we read: "And Michol the daughter of Saul had no child *until* the day of her death". This clearly does not mean either that she gave birth on that day nor, even more obviously, that she did so afterwards.

Nor can the expression of the Vulgate "peperit filium suum primogenitum" (Matt 1:25) imply that after she brought forth her first-born son she might subsequently have had other children. St John Chrysostom says against Helvetius: "Christ was called the first born of Mary not because others were to be born after him, but because no one was born before him". St Paul (Heb 1:6) calls Christ first-born of the Father, which clearly does not imply that the Father would engender more Sons later. And did the Law not command every first-born to be presented in the temple? Was there an exemption if the mother was not to have more children? Thus the translation 'without his having known her she bore a son' is possibly the one that might best reflect the meaning of St Jerome's phrase.

In any case, whichever version one takes, what we are told is that the Virgin Mary conceived without any action on the part of man (*"et incarnatus est de Spiritu Sancto, ex Maria Virgine"* says the Nicene profession of faith). She continued being a virgin in and after birth. This is what the Church teaches, and thus it is.

The silent testimony of her innocence and virginity which Saint Joseph gave on receiving her is commented on by St Bernard: "I, who am weak, would sooner believe in the Resurrection of the Son because of the testimony of Thomas, who doubted and touched, than because of Peter, who heard and believed. I believe in the purity of the mother more easily because of the husband who watched over her than because the Virgin herself defended it with the testimony of her conscience." St Ambrose gives a similar reason of aptitude for the betrothal of Our Lady.

The Virginity of Mary

Theologians have tried to probe deeply into the meaning of this mystery. The piety of the ages has done well to inspire praise for the perfections of Our Lady; and it is meet and just that this should be. At times, though, — as has happened with the apocryphal writings, bearing in mind that even they are no exception — there has been, in some devotional details, more enthusiasm than knowledge of the real conditions within the Holy Family.

The view that Mary's vow of virginity was made in childhood perhaps cannot be maintained. There is ample evidence, nonetheless, to be well satisfied that vows were made by the Jews, even in those days. It was something permitted, regulated and sanctioned by the Law. There were also vows relating to matrimony and conjugal life, vows which once being licit then became obligatory. A vow which affected one's spouse had no value unless the other party was aware of it and approved it. If a man was betrothed to a woman on condition that she had not been previously bound by any vow, and if she having made such a vow were not to disclose it before becoming betrothed, then the betrothal would be invalid. If it was discovered after the wedding (that is, after life in common had begun following the procession to the house of the husband) that the woman had been bound by a vow which she had not declared before the betrothal, the husband was entitled to banish her with a writ of repudiation, *without returning the dowry* (Willam) as a sign of punishment.

Our Lady's question to the Archangel Gabriel "How can this be since I have no knowledge of man?" (Luke 1:34) only makes sense if we suppose she had decided to remain a virgin. If this were not the case, she would have known well enough how it was to be done. But if it was mandatory to declare any vows before the betrothal, and with all the more reason if they affected the other partner, Joseph would have known at this stage of Mary's decision (and whether she had taken a vow respecting it or not) to preserve her virginity and consecration to God. In Palestinian villages virginity did not seem to enjoy any particular esteem, although the celibacy of men was more common and socially more appreciated. Our Lady's consecration to God, then, can only be explained by supposing some supernatural impulse or motion, for it does not seem as if there was a revelation, properly speaking, before the mission of the archangel. "Thus, having considered the various possibilities in her case" — remarks a writer — "the motive of her consecration to God has to be sought in her special situation: she was under the personal direction of God, precisely in so far as she was full of grace. Here is the one and only cause for the consecration of her virginity to God."

As for the rest, the law prescribes certain requirements for this kind of vow for it to be valid. In the case of a maiden, she could not take such a vow before she was twelve years old. If Our Lady did so, it would have been a year or two before her betrothal to Joseph. Thomas Aquinas, with the wisdom and solid common sense which permeates all his works, is of the opinion that Mary had taken a vow. She did so because "works of perfection are more praiseworthy when performed in fulfilment of a vow, and Our Lady was most perfect". But he adds that "the

Mother of God is believed not to have taken an
absolute vow of virginity before being espoused to
Joseph. Although she desired to do so, yet she
yielded her own will to God's judgement" *(Sum Th
III q28 a4)*.

The Implications for Joseph

And Joseph? Here is another sign of the astonish-
ing calibre of this exceptional man. His affection for
Mary must have been very great indeed. He must
have loved her so much and with such generosity of
heart that, learning of her desire to preserve the
consecration she had made to God, he agreed nevertheless to go ahead and pledge his troth, preferring
to renounce having children rather than not to live
with her.

It was also Providential that in the heart of Joseph
so great a love for Mary would be born. God placed
it there so that, afterwards, what He wanted would
take place. It was indeed necessary for Joseph to
love her deeply in order to be able to give up practically everything except her, and to be happy respecting her intimacy with God. It is difficult to think
of a love that is purer, more concerned or more
chaste. It helps us to understand what he had to
suffer thinking he was going to have to renounce her.

And when the angel told him about the mystery of
the Incarnation and about the choice of the two of
them to collaborate jointly in the mystery of the
Redeemer and of salvation, the very great love he
had for his spouse, purified by trial and enriched by
mystery, was sufficient to protect her virginity. St
Thomas values this special characteristic of the marriage of Mary and Joseph to such an extent that he
sees its significance for the whole Church: she "being

a virgin — as St Augustine says — yet is espoused to just one Man, Christ" (*Sum Th* III q29 a1).

Joseph's decision to 'receive' Mary and to celebrate the wedding had an irrevocable character. It meant following through to the end, without considering the possibility of turning back, of retracing steps he had already taken, or of taking any alternative way. It was an abandonment to the Divine will, an unconditional surrender to the service of God, dedicating his life to the Child who was to come and to his Mother. But in no way did relinquishing his life into the hands of God signify — or even imply — passivity. Quite the contrary. It demanded of him a strong fighting spirit and a will ready to tackle every kind of difficulty. The future, or the immediate future at least, was to abound in such hardships. Abandoning one's life . . . what a comfortable expedient it would be if God were then to intervene personally to smooth out all our difficulties, to resolve each problem for us or to overcome every danger or worry. In fact God, once certain of his fidelity, would distance himself from the concerns and anguish of his servant and leave him quite deliberately to the mercy of his own resources — those of a poor man — to face adverse circumstances and the evil and egotism of men.

Joseph responded to every single one of these difficulties. He never complained. He may have felt that these difficulties were the price — a cheap one at that — for the honour and privilege of loving such a wife and of having his love amply and totally reciprocated by her. And later by the Child. There is a prayer to Saint Joseph among those suggested by the Church in preparation for Mass. In it we are reminded of the privilege he was granted "not only to hear and to see God, whom many kings have wished to see but have not seen, to hear but have not heard. He was able to embrace him, to kiss him, to dress him and to look after him". How can one grumble about anything, how can one give even the remotest importance to the relative triviality of this or that when there is absolutely nothing sufficient to repay in the merest way such joy? God did not make an exception of him, at least insofar as the provident care He has for men extends. He did not give Joseph everything, he did not spare him any effort. Nor did he supply what Joseph could and ought to have managed to supply on his own.

Chastity in Marriage

The marriage of Joseph and Mary was, if one may put it this way, the highest possible expression of conjugal love. St Augustine, with his characteristic brilliant wit, which does not mar but adorns his usual profound thinking, considers the twin bases which support the human species — the instinct of conservation on the one hand and that of reproduction on the other. He comments on those men "whose god is their belly" (Phil 3:19) setting about eating and drinking, "placing their whole mind there, as if this were the sole reason for living": these men took "their pleasure and happiness in tasty dishes as an animal takes to his fodder. With reference to conjugal relations", he continues, "lustful men do not approach women for other reasons — with the risk of heavy penalties they reluctantly content themselves with their own wives. It may please God that although they cannot or do not want to renounce lust, they would not allow it to go further than what can be tolerated as a weakness. But if you asked such a man: 'Why do you take a woman?' he would certainly reply, perhaps a little embarrassed, 'to have children, of course'. Let us now suppose that someone, totally worthy of his faith, were to say to him: 'God is powerful enough to raise up children to you, and doubtless he will do so without your having to take a woman'. Caught in this way he would confess that he wasn't really taking a woman in order to have children. May he now confess his infirmity and then take a woman on what was earlier only a pretext: to have children".

This exceptional case, by way of a quite hypothetical example (except in the case of the Virgin Mary), which St Augustine uses, is that of Saint Joseph. His spouse "merited having a child without detriment to her integrity. The same may be applied to her bond with Joseph, which was a true marriage, and a marriage without any loss of virginity. Why then could the chastity of the husband not receive what the chastity of the wife had received?" This would be justified by the magnitude of his love — so noble, so refined, so respectful and with not the slightest admixture of any egoism or search for satisfaction. For true love implies respect. The husband and wife are simply not a pair of animals. Each is made in the image and likeness of God, with an immortal soul and a body which, in a christian, has to be — in St Paul's words — "a temple of God" (I Cor 3:16).

Respect for one's own body and that of one's partner demands chastity. Marriage is not a licence to give free rein to the sexual instinct. Nor can it convert a relationship, in which husband and wife participate in the creative power of God (cooperating with him to bring new lives into the world), into a purely biological or vulgar animality. In marriage, more than ever, there should be respect for the person: it is a relationship between persons, not between a person and a thing. If respect is lost, both for oneself and for one's spouse, love will begin to die at the hands of an egoism which seeks only personal gratification. A man, even when married, has always to be master of his instincts and not ever at their mercy.

Among the texts of the early christian writers, there are very clear statements to show how well those christians cared for the sanctity of marriage. St Justin in his *Apologia* (1,29) writes: "Either we marry from the beginning aiming to procreate children or, by renouncing marriage, we remain absolutely chaste". So common was this way of considering a marriage between christians that Clement of Alexandria, referring to those unions in which a remedy for concupiscence weighed more heavily than its higher objectives, said: "to unite in marriage without any desire for the procreation of children is an insult to nature". Matrimony is not designed to make possible an irregular life of pleasure, nor is it a device for disregarding divine laws. It is not contrary to reason.

An Ideal Worth Fighting For

There are certainly difficult situations in marriage. It is frightening that the scant interior consistency of not a few christians in these times has led to lax and undemanding interpretations with regard to conjugal relations. But what is significant is that in harsher times and for families with fewer resources (for poverty among christians in the early centuries was much commoner than it is today) Lactantius could write: "He who for reasons of poverty cannot bring forth children, may he abstain from the use of mar-

riage, instead of interfering with soiled hands in the
work of God".

It is well to realise that nothing is impossible when
we count on the help of God and when love is strong.
It may not be easy: it will certainly not be comfortable. But it is feasible. To think the opposite is the
same as blaming God for having ordered men (and
not only those who are celibate) to observe a precept
— the sixth — which is impossible. God does not
tantalise anyone. If he commands something it is
because one can fulfil it. "You don't have to be old
or lifeless to practise the virtue of chastity," comments Mgr Escrivá. "Purity comes from love; the
strength and joy of youth are no obstacle for noble
love." And the reason is simple. "This heart of ours"
— he says elsewhere — "was born to love. But when
it is not given something pure, clean and noble to
love it fills itself with squalor" *(Friends of God,*
no. 183).

A man who gets married acquires not only a wife
but also responsibilities. He has also to answer to
God as to how he has built that social pillar which is
the family. What were the foundations and what
were the materials used? No man reaches maturity
until he has committed himself to a cause which is
worth fighting for and becomes a powerful reason (if
not the only one) for living.

We must allude here once more to respect. For the
loss of respect usually coincides with the rejection of
expressions which show it or increase it. Refinement
in mutual dealings and in details of behaviour and
good manners maintain such respect. (Could it be
that familiarity always does bring contempt with it?)
When delicacy disappears, when vulgarity and
coarseness supervene in relations between husband

and wife, replacing the refinement and tenderness of those in love, then something terribly important has been lost. When what fills the heart is not a noble, great and selfless love, then there is limitless room for egoism, meanness and frustration. Here lie the reasons for the breakdown of so many marriages in our times.

From this viewpoint it is now easy to explain the excellence of the marriage of Our Lady and Saint Joseph. Both are filled with the love of God, loving each other with such a deep and noble love that, far from its needing to be nurtured, it fills every moment of the day. So refined and full of respect was their union that it is the real model of what love between the spouses should be.

A certain familiar and facile excuse sometimes bandied about in order to dodge the obligation of such a selfgiving is not valid: it is that she was the Virgin Mary, full of grace, and he was Saint Joseph, a just man. If this reasoning were to be considered legitimate and given sufficient weight, then one would have to deny that Jesus can be any kind of model for us — because he is God!

7

They Met Mary, Joseph and the Child

Mary and Joseph were a young, happily married couple who led a quiet life in Nazareth, a sleepy village of unsophisticated country people. The tranquillity of their life there was unexpectedly disturbed by some news which at any other time would hardly have been worth mentioning. The Emperor Octavius Augustus had issued an edict ordering a census to be taken throughout the Roman Empire. In order to register, all Jews had to return to their own family birthplace, as had been their custom since Moses had converted them into a nation with an exceptional organisation. Joseph, "being of the house and family of David", headed for Bethlehem in Judæa.

Mary and Joseph's decision to make their way there was not made mandatory by the scriptures which said that the Messiah would be born in Bethlehem of David's line; just to comply with the census edict, only Joseph was required to make that particular journey. Did they decide that Our Lady should accompany Joseph and so accomplish the words of scripture? Given the advanced stage of her pregnancy, was Joseph reluctant to leave her alone in Nazareth? Did he for that reason take her with him, without regard to the old familiar writings? The fact is, and remains, that "Joseph went up to Bethlehem from Nazareth" (Luke 2:5).

In Bethlehem there was an inn or tavern — called in the East a *khan* — one of the usual regional 'caravan sites' set aside for travellers. "It consisted of a courtyard surrounded by high walls, frequently with a common well or a pump in the middle, around which jostled or rested chewing camels and braying asses. There were partitions against the walls forming cubicles within which the traveller could leave his bundles and sleeping sack, each cubicle being divided from the others in such a way that the enclosures formed by the partition supports could be rented to those who could pay" (F.W. Willam). It was to one of these 'inns' where travellers used to halt for the night, that Joseph went, only to find there was no room available.

Now if the term 'room' is to be understood simply as a place to settle and unpack, then Joseph had to go elsewhere, since in this case the *khan* could hold no more. It was full as a result of the crowds of travellers who had come to Bethlehem for the census. But if, as occurs in some scriptural passages, we are to understand the word 'room' or 'place' to mean something more fitting, then the expression in the Gospels "there was no room for them at the inn" has a more significant meaning. It is no longer a question of there being vacant space. Even if their lack of money had not prohibited them from competing with

wealthier travellers for slightly less primitive accom-
modation, there was the awkward consideration of
there being no suitably independent enclosure. Suddenly it becomes clear that this whole place was
unsuitable for the Son of God made Man to be born.
Unsuitable, not so much perhaps, for the baby as for
his Mother. What quiet or privacy would Our Lady
have had here for the delicate moment of the delivery of her son? Even if they could have afforded to
stay, such a place would have been separated from
the open courtyard only by a curtain or a tattered
strip of matting. In the noisy yard, only a few paces
away, would sprawl fractious animals, foul-mouthed
camel drivers and no doubt shouting and quite possibly quarreling traders. The constant hubbub of the
crowd, at all hours of the day and night, the comings
and goings of man and beast, all within a few feet of
them. . . . It was no place for this great moment.
Without doubt it was the providential design of God
that no place was found at that inn. A fortunate
accident? His Blessed Son would not be born in the
middle of the vulgarity and dirt of one of those places
of public resort where the Immaculate Virgin would
have been subjected to the inquisitive stare of those
who had nothing to contribute, either of awe or of
yearning, to the splendour of such a moment. Hardship, cold, discomfort . . . yes. A total lack of peace
and dignity, a denial of the right to family intimacy,
squabbling, uproar . . . no.

God provided in another way. Near Bethlehem
there were some caves, the larger ones occasionally
used as stables, where livestock could find refuge
during inclement weather. In some there may have
been a little hay. Certainly, if they had had the
capacity in them for three or four animals, the caves
were large enough to provide shelter for two or three

people if they were in dire straits. And this was
Mary's and Joseph's case.

Maybe some kind soul pointed it out to him, or
perhaps it was Joseph who found the place by himself. The problem was by this time becoming urgent.
It would not resolve itself while worry gnawed at the
mind, fed by an affectionate concern. Neither could
Joseph 'mark time' until the problem became a des-
perate emergency. It does us no good nor does it
serve any useful purpose to allow worries to pile up
within ourselves, fermenting until they explode. This
is not the way to remedy matters. Given that the
'inn' was out of the question, Joseph had diligently
set about finding a suitable place. And, as the solution invariably presents itself when it has been per-
severingly sought, he recognised the answer to his
prayer — it would have to be one of those natural
caves in the rock face. He knew what Our Lady
required, and with his attentive and painstaking
searching, his thoughts focused on the needs of her
approaching confinement. And he discovered the
solution God had prepared, a solution which might
have been overlooked in any other circumstances.

It was no great find, after all. But once swept out
and cleaned, the cave must have proved a much
more wholesome place than the noisy inn with its all
pervasive stink of hot cooking oils and camel dung,
and its continuous confusion and its endless comings
and goings. Here, at least, Our Lady could give birth
in an atmosphere of family togetherness. It would
ensure for her some degree of privacy, and the
decorum required by her modesty and by the greatness of the mystery, even if they would not be
enjoying the best of material conditions.

They remained there until the moment arrived.
(We know it was not long after their arrival in

Bethlehem.) Then "while gentle silence enveloped all things, and night in its swift course was now half gone, the all powerful Word leapt from heaven, from the royal throne" (Wis 18:14-15). Some writers speak of Joseph's refinement, his consideration, of his going outside at the time of the delivery to keep guard at the door, watching over the Child's arrival and respecting the intimate joy of the Mother's first meeting with her infant Son. It is not possible to know. Scripture with its characteristic economy of statement says simply: "When the time had fully come, God sent forth his Son, born of woman, born under the law" (Gal 4:4). And Joseph was there, at that tremendous moment, in that chosen spot, chosen by God to contemplate the prodigious event in such natural normalcy, in the silence and seclusion of the night.

Intimacy with Joseph

"What happened in that stable, in the cavern of rock, had a dimension of profound intimacy; it is something that happens only between a mother and a child being born. No one else is present. Even Joseph, the carpenter from Nazareth, remains a silent witness." Pope John Paul II, in a homily in 1978, alluded profoundly in these words to the depths of the mystery of Bethlehem. Without doubt, from the very beginning, from the very moment itself, the Incarnation of the Son of God implied, as it remains, a uniquely private relationship between Jesus and his Mother. So intense and personal was this newly forged and eternal bond, that all others were excluded; from it a relationship began between these two in which nobody else could participate, with the exception that one man alone was permitted to be a silent witness. And that man was Joseph, a humble man — virtually a nobody, according to the world's judgement.

However, Joseph's own real bond of closeness with Jesus was of another order, differing in kind from that between the Son and his Mother. Mary's was maternal. Joseph's knowledge that he was outside the mystery must have induced in him an inspired respect, requiring his imposing on himself certain limits of conduct which, being a just man, he would never have crossed. The Virgin Mary, because of who she was, could go much further in exceeding these limits. It was she in fact, and not Joseph, who was able to say without as much as a look of reproach from Jesus some years later: "Son, why have you behaved like this towards us?" And many years later still, she spoke quietly to the waiters: "Do what He tells you . . .", without the slightest doubt of what Jesus would do.

The great event concerned, above all else, the Mother and her Son. Joseph was to participate shortly afterwards, when the profound and mysterious relationship had already been established between Jesus and His Mother. Initially, Joseph's participation in the mystery had come about through the knowledge given him by the angel's revelation of the mission he was to carry out for these two exceptional people. Apart from his involvement in discharging his assigned task, the part he had to play as the husband of Mary bound him to Jesus in a degree superior to that of any other creature. Joseph had not previously been asked to agree, as had Our Lady, since when he became aware of the truth about her pregnancy, he was already related to the mystery by virtue of their betrothal. From then onwards, in all that responded to their role, and in all that concerned the mission to which he had been called, Joseph was a silent witness.

His was a witness not intended to give to the world faith in the truth he knew; it was not to communicate the news to others. The purpose of his witness was simply to contemplate it. Other witnesses (not silent ones) would later seek out Jesus in order in future years to be witness to the things they had seen or heard, to be witness to his teachings, to his miracles, and in particular to his Resurrection. Joseph was not called to be this kind of witness. He had not been asked to communicate anything to anybody. It would be sufficient for him to be present, to accompany Jesus and Mary; he was never to leave them alone.

So he was there when he was needed, silent, attentive, strongly dependable and loving. He was on hand for his wife to show him their son, the Son of God made Man; the son was his Lord. Joseph was the first to gaze upon and to adore the Child who had come to Earth 'in such a wondrous way', the astounding truth of which he knew as did only one other. Nonetheless, to say nothing? Not even a whisper to anyone about the inexpressible happiness of being able to hold the Redeemer of the World in his hands?

Later he was also to be the silent and delighted witness of the arrival of the shepherds, who having seen and heard the angels announce: "I bring glad tidings of great joy to you and all mankind" (Luke 2:10), said to one another: "Let us go over to Bethlehem and see this thing that has happened and which the Lord has made known to us" (Luke 2:15).

He saw them approach the cave, timid and curious, to see for themselves the "babe wrapped in swaddling clothes" (Luke 2:12). He heard them explain to the Virgin about the apparition of the angel who had told them about the birth of the Saviour in Bethlehem, about the sign by which they would recognise him, describing how a multitude of angels had gathered with this first messenger, glorifying God and promising "peace on earth to men of good will". He was a happy witness of all of this, without being too astonished. He had not heard the vast company of angels chorusing God's praises, but his experience taught him that what the shepherds said was not only possible but certainly true. He too could recount something similar about the effects on his soul of God's words announced by the angel. Peace came first of all, but a peace the world could not give, as Jesus was to say later. Then, a profound sense of joy, of calm, an inexpressibly intense emotion of the spirit. Of course, his was not a joy as easily communicated as that of the shepherds: ". . . and all who heard it wondered at what the shepherds told them" (Luke 2:18). Joseph would discuss his secret only with Our Lady. But his joy was no less ecstatic. Since he kept it in his heart, perhaps it lasted longer.

Joseph also contemplated the radiant happiness of the woman who was his wife, this marvellous lady who had been entrusted into his keeping. Enthralled by the way she gazed at her Son, he saw her own marvellous joy, her own overflowing love, her every gesture so full of exquisite tenderness and meaning.

And the Child was the Only Son of God, who revealed himself to men "in that little body, like one of us, a tiny infant, totally fragile and vulnerable. Subject to man's whims, yet entrusted to his love without the slenderest means of defence, He weeps and the world feels nothing; it is not capable of feeling anything. For the cry of a newborn infant can only be heard at a few paces!" (John Paul II). Nevertheless this baby is dependent on the unshakeable love of one man, rather than being at the mercy of mankind's unpredictable attention. Joseph, that honourable man who had been chosen as Mary's husband, was to watch over the defenceless boy who had been born into this world's history. Joseph's strength had to supply for the weakness of the fragile child, a child incapable of knowing the worth of this quiet man, but who had wanted to be dependent on his utter fidelity, to rest in his arms, toughened by work but gentle and full of loving care.

Joseph could hear the Child's first cry. He was close by whilst all around was silent. Ever present and attentive, he would be quick to respond. He was there to be of service to Him and to his Mother, to be at their beck and call. He took his responsibility so seriously that he was never far from them.

To tell the truth, his mind was never far enough away from Jesus to forget about him even momentarily. He knew that the reason for his own existence was that this Child depended on him with total trust. It was the same trust manifested by every newborn infant that is . . . helpless.

Concern for Children

Perhaps we can discover why in our day we do not seem to be sensitive to the vulnerability of this Child. We are never sufficiently near to hear him laugh or cry, to look at his eyes and to guess from his facial expression whether he needs something; we are not close enough to understand that he is perhaps thanking us for some little service or just for the pleasure of our company, or sometimes to suspect that he is perhaps reproaching us for our coldness and indifference. We cannot see him or hear him because we have distanced ourselves from him. Could it be, perhaps, that we have turned our backs and are looking the other way?

Today, unfortunately, such an attitude towards Him is all too common. We are repeatedly told that our modern world living out the final decades of the second christian millenium is hungry for God. Maybe so. If such is the case this 'hunger' is so well concealed that the very opposite has every appearance of being true. It would seem that men are not too deeply concerned about the Child born in Bethlehem "when a great silence came down upon all things". If we look closely at our newspapers we get the distinct impression that there is a compassion for children — in the abstract. It appears that our world does not like babies very much. The method it has adopted to stop them crying is to stop them being born. Our generation has shown great ability in administering and evaluating such arbitrary procedures and in analysing their results. Perhaps we today are so remote from all of this, so wholeheartedly involved in other things, that there just isn't the time to stand back and appreciate the marvel a child is supposed to be. But do not millions of us turn our eyes away and refuse to see the human child as fragile, feeble, helpless and in total need? Its defencelessness does not give us sleepless nights, nor does it cause us to lose our 'civilised' outlook. Perhaps it is a justifiable fear — a fear people have that thinking about children will make them lose their egoism and perhaps even lead them to change their life-style. We do not know. But, in practice, our modern preference seems to be for products, for what money can buy, for previously dispensable luxuries — in fact, for anything instead of children.

A Contemplative in the World

On the other hand, for the couple in that cavern hewn out of rock, the presence of a Child somehow made irrelevant all the commodities they were short of. When all was said and done, He was what they had. And in such a situation who would remember the missing things? What could one miss? Today, we risk missing the chance to become masters of the goods of the Earth. There is no limit to what some people want of this world. This is folly. For it is commonly known that our appreciation is enhanced by having less of something rather than more. A little warmth gives greater comfort than a furnace of fire. A gentle breeze brings more relief than will a howling hurricane. Men seem to have lost all sense of proportion; they are never satisfied with what they have, for nothing seems sufficient for them. Through not knowing to say 'enough!' to the flood of ephemeral 'necessities', they sometimes find these same necessities converted into weighty burdens. Stumbling around with similar foolish loads, they find themselves destroying their capacity to contemplate God. He reveals Himself to us constantly, even through the tiny daily occurrences like a child's cry, and the smile and the striving sounds of a baby when it seems to be trying to say something.

We may well feel frustrated when we do not achieve this or that new ambition. Or our pride is hurt if we have to trail behind others. This so concerns us that we have to ignore everything else, and at times we are compelled to ignore everybody else. Gone is our interior peace and joy.

Joseph, on the other hand, from the shadows and without making a show of it, sees the adoration of the Child, the deference to the Mother with no recognition of his own role, as both fitting and normal. Here lies in no small part his grandeur: he expects nothing for himself. But when it comes to giving, he is the first to offer. In his shouldering of responsibility, at his work and in fulfilling his obligations, he is an active participant.

It is also true that when he limits himself to a passive role he is an unusual spectator. Far from merely watching, he contemplates. To contemplate is to watch with joy and self-giving. Joseph is contemplative and he contemplates Jesus; his contemplation is practical and direct, not mystical. He contemplates not a glorified Jesus but a helpless Jesus. Thus his contemplation leads to action, because the helplessness of the Infant calls for the help of men. It calls to action, not to activism; for activism is incompatible with contemplation, which is always serene. All calm is destroyed by the turbulence that accompanies thoughtless activity. The activist goes at it as if the outcome of his feverish activities depended on him alone and as if he were running out of time.

The reality is that we are living in a poverty-stricken epoch. There is such a vacuum in the souls of men, such a cascade of empty chatter and streams of useless information that they are being submerged by it. Really useful information is what the shepherds received from the angel: "Today a Saviour is born to you". Not empty words but words replete with content, meaningful, alive and vivifying; for the Child who lies in the manger is none other than the Word of God made flesh. And this one man — Joseph — lives such an enriched interior life that he is the model for contemplatives in the world; he is the force on whom the Child and his Mother rely with absolute confidence.

8

"You Shall Name Him Jesus"

After the Birth and before the Magi arrived to adore the newborn King of the Jews, St Luke mentions two events in which Joseph must certainly have fulfilled a role, although characteristically, he is not mentioned by name. It was a hidden role, almost a routine one, a function fulfilled by every father in Israel. While it is unlikely to help us get to know Saint Joseph better, it could perhaps teach us something. It may even help us to get to know ourselves better.

These matters which St Luke deals with at unequal length are the circumcision and the presentation of Jesus in the temple. If the latter seems to take on a greater importance, this is due among other reasons to the intervention of the old man Simeon. He prophesied about Jesus and his Mother in Joseph's presence. The narrative is consequently more extensive than that of the circumcision and has proportionately more details of fact.

Every male child was officially integrated into the chosen people through the rite of circumcision. This was the sign of God's alliance and covenant with his people. It dated back to Abraham to whom the Lord had said: "This is my covenant which you shall keep, between me and you and your descendants after you. Every male among you shall be circumcised" (Gen 17:10-12).

St Matthew omits this moment of Jesus' infancy. St Luke sums it up very briefly: "When the eighth day came and the child was to be circumcised, they gave him the name Jesus, the name the angel had given him before his conception" (Luke 2:21).

Circumcision was a highly significant event in the life of a child. So important was it considered that it even took precedence over the law of rest on the sabbath. Only if a child was in danger of death could there be sufficient reason to defer it. It was important for a double reason: on being incorporated through the rite of circumcision into the chosen people whom God had formed, (for not to be circumcised was to tear up the pact and be excluded from the people), he was made a sharer and participant of the promise. What is more, he would even, in a certain sense, become part of the deposit of tradition and become responsible in his turn for passing it on. With the imposition of the name, the child began its own life as if it were now for the first time being itself, with its own unique and distinctive personality.

The ceremony took place not in the synagogue but in the house where the child lived with his parents. The minister of circumcision was a practitioner or surgeon, skilled at his task, and responsible for performing it. He did so in the father's name. Witnesses and a sponsor were needed. It followed a specific rite in which the father was briefly involved. The minister of the circumcision would say: "Blessed is God our Lord, who blessed us with his precepts and commanded this circumcision". The father of the child would then reply: "He blessed us with his precepts and commanded us to introduce the child to the covenant of Abraham our father".

After the circumcision the naming took place. As both ceremonies took place at home, relatives were usually present. It is unlikely that there was a big celebration in Jesus' case for, if they had relatives in Bethlehem, Mary would hardly have had to give birth in a stable. As there are no facts available, it is easy to understand that there is no agreement on whether the circumcision took place where Jesus was born and where for the moment Mary and Joseph took refuge, or in another house in Bethlehem to which they may have moved. St Epiphanus is inclined to favour the former.

The Significance of *His* Name

At the imposition of the name, the father, as head of the family, had an important function. It was he who gave the name as he had authority in the family. He would say who, in his eyes, the new member of the chosen people was to be, for every name signified something. But in this case there is some doubt, for St Luke says that it was not Joseph, as head of the family, who gave the name of Jesus. Instead *"they gave* him the name Jesus, the name the angel had given him before his conception".

"They gave". Who did? The reference is necessarily to Joseph and Mary, for no other person had anything to do with it. In the revelation of God's plan for Our Lady at the annunciation, the archangel had said "and you will give birth to a son whom you shall name Jesus". Both father and mother then had been given the task of naming the Child. It was not to be a name they chose, nor any name tailored to their tastes and preferences, but precisely the one the angel had revealed. It was a name which revealed who the Child really was and what all this would mean for the chosen people — *Jesus,* that is to say, *Saviour.* He had to save men; he was to be the cause of their salvation.

According to general opinion relatives and friends were not at the ceremony as it took place a long distance away from Nazareth where they normally lived. With only a few new acquaintances there, it would not be fitting for Mary to do something so assertive as to place herself on par with the head of the family in a society where each had a well defined place, and give, along with Joseph, the name which the father himself ought to have presented.

It is generally noted that both Jesus and Mary, although not subject to the law, followed its requirements. Not only is the circumcision a good example of this, but so is the presentation of Jesus in the temple and the purification of Our Lady. Referring to the circumcision, St Thomas gives good reasons why it was convenient for Jesus to subject himself to the law. To show, for example, that he had a body of flesh; to prove that he was of Abraham's lineage; to deny any excuse to those who would not wish to recognise him on the ground or pretext that he was uncircumcised; to submit to the Law so that we ourselves might learn to obey . . . ; and so also that "this should be imitated by us, in fulfilling those things which are of obligation in our own time" (*Sum Th* III q37 a1 ad2). Later, Fr Isidoro of Isolano, in the first half of the sixteenth century, would write

The Greatest of the Gifts of Saint Joseph. Commenting on the "gift of the imposition of the most holy name of Jesus", he reasons thus: as it was the custom for the father who had the authority to give his son a name, it follows that the Father named his Son at his incarnation. This name was revealed to Mary by the archangel Gabriel, and by an angel to Joseph. On presenting the name, Joseph "revealed a divine secret to the world, taking the place of the heavenly Father". Isidoro ends by quoting a *Commentary* on St Luke: "It was not fitting for such a glorious name to be first uttered by just any man, but by the most excellent being, so that no man would feel he was its author. For the same reason it was fitting that he who would impose the name would be more excellent than the rest". With this, one realises how God sees the worth of Joseph.

The Importance of Names

Today, we give little real importance to names. Why should it be important if it is only to distinguish one person from another? In baptism it is usual to give the name of the father or mother or of one or other of the grandparents. (It was a custom among the Jews also to look for a name among relatives, as one sees in the Gospel when it comes to naming John the Baptist.) Other possibilities we are familiar with are the name of the saint whose feast is on the date of birth or to whom the parents have a particular devotion. At times a name is chosen simply because one likes the sound of it. In any case, a name has generally little to relate about the person who bears it. It is not surprising that frequently a nickname better describes a person than his own name does. It does not indicate his essence but it usually shows some characteristic trait. If we say Claire or Nina, Russell or Matthew, we don't indicate any particular characteristics of those who bear these names, except perhaps to show that one is speaking of a man or a woman. But if in referring to someone we say 'lofty', 'freckles', 'gabby' or 'handy', then we are pointing to someone who is characterised by a quality sufficiently perceptible to distinguish that person from others with the same name. It is so special that it is invariably sufficient to indicate who the person is.

The truth is that names exist, in principle at least, to indicate what a thing — or a person — is. "A name should answer to the nature of a thing" says Thomas Aquinas (*Sum Th* III q37 a2). Aristotle in his *Metaphysics* declares that "a concept signified by a name is its definition". A name is significant; it signifies something. When one reads in Genesis (2:19 *et seq*) that Adam gave a name to each animal, what he did was to say what each was. And when he saw his wife, he called her *woman* — taken from *man* (Gen 2:23) — designating her by her nature. But when the name comes from God, then this name has a profound relationship with what that man is in his deepest reality, with what is most essential, with what goes to make up his being. This can be seen often. There are several cases, for example, like that of Hosea. God commanded him to name his children after the relationship between God and these people: "Call him *No-people-of-mine,* because you are not my people and I am not your God" (Hos 1:9). We can also look at Abraham. He was Abram until God changed his name to ratify his alliance with Him. "Behold my covenant is with you, and you shall be the father of a multitude of nations. No longer shall you be Abram, but Abraham, for I have made you the father of a multitude of nations" (Gen 17:5). In the case of the last of Jacob's sons, Benjamin (*son of the right hand*, the name given him by Jacob) was previously Benoni (*son of my sorrow*, the name given him by his mother Rachel) (Gen 35:18).

Thus the name Jesus, meaning Saviour, indicated who Jesus was. Here there is a deep unity between the person of Jesus and his mission. His name is holy and has the virtue of not having been previously given to another person. Having been humiliated and "made obedient unto death, even death on a cross", God "highly exalted him and bestowed on him the name which is above every name; that at the name of Jesus every knee should bow, in heaven and on the earth and under the earth" (Phil 2:8-10).

In the name of Jesus the Nazarene Peter commanded the cripple at the gate of the temple which is called Beautiful: "Walk!" (Acts 3:6). When the priests, elders and scribes got together on the following day to ask him to give an account of what had happened, they enquired: "By what power or by what name did you do this? Peter, filled with the Holy Spirit", with due respect for the authorities but with simplicity and clarity, replied: "Be it known to you all and to all the people of Israel that by the name of Jesus Christ of Nazareth . . . . this man is standing before you well." In the name of this Jesus, whom they had crucified, of the rejected stone which had now become the cornerstone. "There is salvation in no one else; for there is no other name under heaven among men by which we must be saved" (Acts 4:12). His is a name to be adored because he is salvation. His name specifies what Jesus is — the Saviour. There is none other.

God Has Given Each Person a Name

If each man is unique and unrepeatable; if each one is called to life and is born with a variety of talents; if throughout one's existence God keeps granting each man or woman a series of graces, all this is not pure chance or capriciously distributed by God. It relates to the plan God has had *ab æterno* for the universe, and more specifically, for the Redemption. If a name has a reason for being, in specifying what all things are, God ought to have a name for every one of them. Perhaps when we talk about human beings it might be better to say that each person has a unique and unrepeatable name, known to God. It indicates what he or she *is* in God's eyes, both in connection with the specific goal for which He gave the gift of life and in relation to the Redemption. This name, which only God knows, expresses what is most profound, personal and essential in each one. Here is where the identity of a person lies. For most men it has little to do either with the image others may see or with what one thinks of oneself. It is not a name that fits the image, mask or disguise — this false personality which we have acquired through original sin and through personal sin, a bogus identity constructed in a lifetime by the continual strengthening of the 'old man' thanks to the affirmation 'I'. It corresponds rather to the genuine *being* which lies beneath this disguise, under this mask and image, and which with the help of grace, gradually begins to show through by the effects of the cross of Christ. He who denies himself in order to affirm Jesus Christ and submit to Him, he who does not fear risking his life to win it, he who is capable of burying himself and dying like a grain of wheat: such a person is capable of getting rid of the

false crust of seeming, the dissimulating shell of arti-
ficiality, the unfortunate inheritance left us by Adam.
Gradually one discovers the being, restored by grace,
which each one is in the mind of God.

The name we bear and by which we are known is
fictitious, contrived and conventional. Only God
knows what we really are. Only he truly knows us
and can call us by the name which is most appropriate for us. "Ego vocavi nomine tuo: meus es tu; I
have called by your name: you are mine" (Is
43:1). One day we too will learn this name. We will
then know who we really are, what is our own
identity, because this name will identify the essence
of our being. "To him who conquers I will give some
of the hidden manna. I will give him a white stone,
with a new name written on the stone which no one
knows except him who receives it" (Rev 2:17). No
one, except God and him who receives it. For, as St
Thomas says, if no one can reach the essence of
things, neither can anyone give each thing its *essential name* — that which truly expresses its ultimate
and deepest reality: what it is in the mind of God.

This new name which one can really call one's
own, so corresponds to the new man restored by
Christ, that it will be fit to appear beside the divine
name. Such is the power of the Saviour. "He who
proves victorious I will make into a pillar in the
sanctuary of my God and he will stay there forever. I
will inscribe on him the name of my God, and on
him the name of the city of my God, the new
Jerusalem which comes down from my God in
heaven, and on him my own new name for him as
well" (Rev 3:12). There is even more to it, because
this new name will have such substance and conform
so well to the saving designs of God and be so
reconciled with the Saviour that there comes further

explicit recognition that it is everlasting: "He who proves victorious will be dressed in white robes. I shall not blot his name out of the book of life: I will confess his name in the presence of my Father" (Rev 3:5).

But it is essential to be victorious. This new name is always linked with him who wins, bearing in mind that it refers to the winner in the eyes of God and not to the one so considered in the eyes of men. The victor is he who, above all, achieves victory over himself, and over the world, the devil and the flesh. He is a winner in the same category as Joseph of Nazareth, who overcame the forces of evil in everything which opposed the divine will, everything which tried to prevent the complete fulfilment of the mission God had given him. His life was such a victory that his death was the birth of life. It is only those living who will have a name, a new name. Those condemned will have no such name for they will lack an identity. Although they exist they shall not live, for they have attained what the *Apocalypse* calls "a second death" — which is eternal death.

Those words of the *Apocalypse* which say "I know all about you: how you are reputed to be alive and yet are dead" (Rev 3:1) can be applied with justice to many in the world. Exactly the opposite happened to Joseph. In the eyes of the world he did not exist. A carpenter in a village, barely known in that quiet corner as one among the many who lived there. His work did not spread beyond the limits of a small locality. He was such an ordinary person that he lived as merely one more in the anonymity of the multitude who were just as ordinary as he was. Behold then, as time goes on, his growing stature. The extraordinary calibre of this just man becomes brighter, more and more luminous as the centuries pass. He did not count for anything, and unlike many, seemed to carry the name of death, of non-existence. Nevertheless he lived facing God with an intensity the world could not imagine, and in such a way that he was chosen to impose a name by Him through whom we all live. This is why he now has a new name, which only God and he know. For him it is a reason for glory.

9

Simeon Blessed Them

The presentation of Jesus in the Temple and the purification of Our Lady constituted two distinct and independent ceremonies and conformed with separate precepts of the Law. The ritual presentation signified the expression of God's right over every first-born male, as Exodus (13:1,2) commanded: "The Lord said to Moses, 'consecrate to me all the first-born, whatever is the first to open the womb among the people of Israel, both of man and of beast is mine'." The first-born was not only to be sanctified and consecrated to God but also to be redeemed — that is to say, bought back. "Every first-born of man among your sons you shall redeem. And when in time to come your son asks you 'What does this mean?' you shall say to him, 'By strength of hand the Lord brought us out of Egypt, from the house of bondage. For when Pharaoh stubbornly refused to let us go, the Lord slew all the first-born in the land of Egypt, both the first-born of man and the first-

born of cattle. Therefore I sacrifice to the Lord all
the males that first open the womb, but all the
first-born of my sons I redeem' " (Exodus 13:13-15).

The first-born belonged to God on two counts.
They belonged to him before all else as "first fruits"
(because all the first fruits — crops and animals, as
well as men — had to be offered to God as an
acknowledgement of His dominion over all His creatures). They also were specially His as prospective
heads of families, since it was these same first-born
who, in a patriarchal society, carried out the office of
priest, in the sense that it fell to them to offer
sacrifice and to ensure continuity in the worship of
God. When God decreed that this priesthood should
be exercised by men of the tribe of Levi, he told
Moses how many they should be. "Number all the
first-born males of the people of Israel, from a month
old and upward, taking their number by names. And
you shall take the Levites for me instead of all the
first-born among the people of Israel" (Num
3:40-41). Since the number of first-born sons among
the people of Levi would far exceed the number of
priests required, God commanded their 'redemption' with "five silver shekels for each".

It was not written down within what period of time
the consecration and the subsequent buying-back of
the first-born son should take place.

Just as the presentation concerned the son, so did
the purification affect the mother. When a woman
gave birth to a son she remained, for the seven days
following the birth in need of ritual purification
under the Law. On the eighth day, the child was
circumcised. "And after that she must wait for
thirty-three days more . . . touching nothing that is
hallowed, and never entering the sanctuary until the
time is up" (Lev 12:1 *et seq*). When this period was

over, she had to be 'purified' through the offering of
"a lamb of one year old as a burnt-sacrifice, and a
young pigeon or a turtle dove by way of amends". If
the family were too poor and could not afford to
offer a lamb, then another turtle-dove or pigeon
could take its place. One of these was to be offered
as a burnt-sacrifice, and one by way of amends. Now
at the priest's intercession she would be 'purified'.
The mother's presence at the ceremony was not
indispensable; the husband, or even a third person,
could offer the sacrifice.

When, as in the case of Mary and Joseph, the
couple were living near Jerusalem (Bethlehem was
some five miles or so distant), and even though going
to the Temple was not absolutely necessary for fulfilling either of the two precepts, pious Jews would go
up to the Holy Place in order to fulfil the Law. In this
way "when the time had come for purification . . .
they brought him up to Jerusalem, to present him
before the Lord there. It is written in God's Law,
that whatever male offspring opens the womb is to be
reckoned sacred to the Lord; and so they must offer
in sacrifice for him, as God's law commanded, a pair
of turtle-doves, or two young pigeons" (Luke
2:22-24). Unnoticed among the other young couples
who were also bringing their sons, Mary and Joseph
would have made their way through the Eastern (or
"Beautiful") gate of the Temple. From here they
would have gone through the inner gate that led into
the Court of the Jews. Here the priest would be
awaiting the arrival of the parents who were coming
to present their first-born sons. He would then proceed with the ceremonial purification of the mother.

It fell to the father to carry out the double duty of
presentation and redemption. It was Joseph then
who undertook to fulfil this rite, which signified not

only the consecration to God of the first-born, but
also commemorated God's merciful action on behalf
of His people. He had freed them from captivity and
servitude even to the extent of overcoming Pharaoh's resistance by destroying the first-born of the
Egyptians. Finally, he had dispensed them from
service in the priestly or Levitical office by means of
the payment of the five silver pieces.

But by no means, as far as the Holy Family were
concerned, was everything the same as with the
others. In the first place, Jesus, being who He was,
was not subject to the Law, but above it. Nor had
Mary need of any kind of purification, because she
had conceived, given birth, and remained a spotless
virgin. In spite of this, and inasmuch as these marvels
were not common knowledge, they scrupulously
fulfilled the Law as if the Mother and her Child were
not the Lady who was full of grace and the very
Author of grace Himself. It would not be right that
people should afterwards be able to say of Jesus that
he had broken the Law, or of the Blessed Virgin that
she remained legally impure.

A Holy and Perfect Sacrifice

But if the presentation of Jesus had in this case a
hidden meaning, since He had come to consecrate to
his Father not only his life, his death and his resurrection, but also all human endeavours which,
through Him and from Him, would receive a special
fitness to be raised above their purely natural significance, that meaning did not in any way extend to the
ritual redemption. Strictly speaking, He was not
redeemed; or if He was, it could only have been in
the sense in which the first-born were consecrated
to God in the Old Law. Jesus exercised a unique

function, being the fountainhead of all priesthood as such, and of His high Priesthood; the priesthood under the Law of those who went before Him was simply a figure. He came, as Eternal Priest, to offer Himself as a holocaust for sin, and to redeem mankind from the power of Satan.

So Joseph, although he was not a priest, was the first to offer to God a holy and perfect sacrifice, the Word become incarnate in the womb of Mary, his spouse, an offering of infinite value such as the world had never seen. It appeared as though God had arranged things so that the last of the Patriarchs would undertake once more to fulfil the priest-like role of his ancient predecessors, before God had established the priesthood of Aaron and the Levites. Joseph offered to God the Messiah, whose independence from the levitical priesthood was now made clear. The infant Saviour was ransomed by the five shekels that his father had earned, one by one, with the work of his hands. Joseph had assumed the care of the One who was going to perfect the worship of God through the sacrifice. It would now be offered throughout the whole world "from the rising of the sun to its going down". Thus, on this occasion, the ceremony of the Presentation reflected and heralded and did not simply prefigure the reality. A new priesthood had begun.

An event of enormous significance took place in the Temple before the ceremony, when the child Jesus was brought in by his parents. "There was a man named Simeon living in Jerusalem, an upright man of careful observance, who waited patiently for comfort to be brought to Israel," writes St Luke. "The Holy Spirit was upon him" (Luke 2:25). He must have been a man of prayer for the Holy Spirit to have marked him out so completely, even to the point of fulfilling what was the highest hope of all good Israelites. It was his own hope too, because he had lived all the years of his life anxiously awaiting the Saviour whose coming had been foretold. Indeed, "by the Holy Spirit it had been revealed to him that he was not to meet death until he had seen that Christ whom the Lord had anointed". He was led by the Spirit Himself into the Temple on the very day on which Mary and Joseph were bringing the Child to carry out what the Law required.

It was with surprise and not a little astonishment that they would see, on entering, a venerable old man step forward to meet them. He stretched out and gently took the Child in his arms. In this way he gave public witness of the presence of the Redeemer among men, blessing God for having fulfilled the promise that He had made him: "My own eyes have seen that saving power of Thine which Thou hast prepared in the sight of all nations" (Luke 2:31). He then also blessed Mary and Joseph. Addressing the Virgin, he revealed in prophetic words what the Holy Spirit had made known to him concerning the Child and his Mother.

It has been observed and can be quite clearly seen even without particularly close study — that St Matthew, in dealing with the childhood of Jesus, brings major attention to bear on Joseph, while St Luke centres more on the Virgin Mary. Thus, since it is the latter evangelist who narrates these events for us, Our Lady appears in the forefront. This is highlighted by Simeon's prophecy being directed to her alone. Nor is there an explicit mention of Saint Joseph at this point. He was there, nevertheless, watching and listening.

He knew how Simeon, perhaps with the Child still in his arms, turned to Mary and looked at her. He heard how, in contrast to the glorious future the old man had predicted for the Child ("a light that shall give revelation to the Gentiles . . . glory of thy people Israel . . ."), the veil was drawn back a little to reveal the shadow of the cross. This little Child was destined to be "a rock of scandal and a sign of contradiction", to spell ruin for some and salvation for others. In a mysterious way his mother herself would have to share in this destiny. Joseph had already fully grasped this special, and indeed unique, bond that united the two of them. What may well have appeared inevitable to him, and in the nature of things only to be expected, even though it would be painful for him to contemplate, was that if the son had to suffer, so would the Mother suffer with him, 'in compassion'. That union of Mother and Child, expressed with such intimate perfection in the joy of the conception, of the birth in Bethlehem and of the peaceful Nazareth years, could not be broken by pain.

A Lesson in Humility

Throughout this scene which St Luke has presented to us, Joseph's role may appear to casual human scrutiny to be a secondary one. It does not matter — nor can it be perceived from St Luke's narrative — that it was he who presented the Child, he who paid the ransom. We know this from our knowledge of the Jewish people's religious customs. Once again, Joseph is presented to us almost as a spectator, even when we know he must have taken a leading role in the events that took place in the Temple.

Yet here, once again, there is neither mere chance in the choice of what is to be narrated, nor are there

any superfluous words; there is nothing merely fortuitous, no artistic or imaginative colouring in the
sacred author's selection of details or in his way of
presenting them. As it happens, it does not appear to
have mattered at all to Saint Joseph whether he
fulfilled a role which seemed to place him in background obscurity or, indeed, any other role, if it
came to that, so long as it was what God wanted of
him.

Such an attitude — habitual in him, one would say
— that of remaining in silence, that of quietly contemplating from the shadows all that concerned the
Son and the Mother, also carries a lesson for us from
which we may· profit if we know how to apply it to
our own lives. For this humble man never did anything to attract attention to himself (something that
we — at least most of us — cannot say of ourselves),
nor was he in the slightest concerned as to whether
posterity would hear anything of him or not. At-
tending to what he had to do, he did not have time
for immature preoccupation with himself. His humility freed him from that type of leprosy which
attacks men, or some men, to the point of disfigure-
ment; the disease of obsessive preoccupation with
one's own doings or one's own reputation. To what
lengths will some people not go to preserve intact
and untarnished their artificial 'image'?

Joseph: a man indistinguishable from others and
the last person to attract the attention of his contemporaries; a man who passed unnoticed among other
men, and content to be no more than what he was.
This is what really matters. There are men who need
to be perpetually on display: they have to make a
show of their talents, their courage, their intelligence, their abilities, their character or their competence; they are incapable of believing themselves

of some worth unless others affirm this by means of public recognition and applause. They do not appear to be completely convinced of their own existence unless they see their names in the paper, or unless everybody is speaking about them. They need to see themselves reflected in others, as in a mirror, in order to assure themselves that they indeed *are,* as if their very personalities were dependent on advertising. A man's personality, however, resides, in what he *is,* not in what he possesses, or in what others think or say of him. It is not something that lies outside of himself, but in the centre of his being.

It is almost a matter of experience as Thomas Merton has observed, that "the greatest freedom is to be found in the exercise of humility. As long as one has to defend the imaginary being who is felt to be important" he says, "peace of heart will be lacking. When that phantasm is compared with the contrived images of others, all joy will be lost, since one will have begun to deal with what is unreal, and there is no joy in things that do not exist". Joseph did not have to put up a defence of any imaginary being; he did not feel obliged to compare himself with anybody else. He had other more important things to concentrate on. He would never have considered himself a failure for being, humanly speaking, less than others, or for not being able to offer his spouse a public prestige that would fill her with admiration and vanity. He was never saddened by being no more than he was, or by not being anything else. "True humility, I really believe," says St Teresa in *The Way of Perfection,* "consists to a great extent in being ready for what the Lord desires to do with us, in being happy that He should go ahead and do it, and in always considering ourselves unworthy to be called His servants."

The humble man has a quality that is difficult to find in any other sort of person: it is a readiness to accept his own state in life without bitterness, without sadness or resentment. When in *The Imitation of Christ* the Lord speaks to his servant Thomas à Kempis and tells him how he must be tried and tested, He specifies the ways in which the soul will be proved: "You must often do things for which you have no inclination, and give up other things that you want to do. The things that please other people will go well; what pleases you will make no progress. What others say will be heard with attention; what you say will be thought worthless. Others will ask and will receive, you will ask and get nothing. Others will be much spoken of and praised; you will be passed over in silence. Others will be entrusted with one task or another, but you will be thought good for nothing. Your old nature will sometimes find this painful, and it is a great thing if you can endure it in silence."

This enduring silence has great merit. But the true moral worth of the humble man lies precisely in the naturalness with which he accepts that he should not be spoken of, that attention should not be paid to him, that he should not be regarded as of much use, that he should not be listened to, that he should find nothing to complain about in putting up with what others would see as being held in contempt. The poor and the humble do not think about themselves. They yield precedence with ease. They accept the things that go wrong as a normal part of life, a part, in fact, of great value for them, and each little joy fills them with an immense happiness for which just as with rebuffs and contradictions, they show themselves truly grateful.

10

"Get Up and Escape Into Egypt . . ."

When St Matthew gives in his gospel his account of the adoration of the Magi, he leaves out the name of Joseph: "And so, going into the dwelling, they found the child there with his mother Mary and fell down to worship him" (Matt 2:11). The omission does not necessarily imply that Joseph was not there; what it certainly does mean is that Jesus was with his mother, that she was holding him in her arms. Since the main emphasis in this part of St Matthew's narrative is on the arrival and the adoration of the Magi, it would have been superfluous to mention anyone else who happened to be in the house at the time. There may well have been, apart from Joseph, a crowd of neighbours. The arrival from a distant country of such celebrities, coming to visit a young mother in a poor little house, not to mention their conspicuously outlandish retinue, could scarcely have passed without notice. We may say with confidence that Joseph is not mentioned as taking part in this event simply because he had no role to play. The very opposite is true in the case of what happens next.

King Herod had shown himself courteously well disposed towards the Magi. When they reached Jerusalem they seem to have no difficulty in being admitted to his presence. Ingenuously asking Herod where they could find the One born to be king of the Jews, they understandably caused consternation. Herod, thrown into confusion, went to the length of summoning the priests and scribes to enquire from them what they made of the Magi's question. When they advised him about its possible significance and pointed out that the village of Bethlehem had always been designated as the future cradle of the Messiah, Herod had the Magi called to him. He saw them off on their way to the place indicated, not without first, however, having carefully verified the time of the star's first sighting. Nevertheless, in exchange for the trouble he had taken, he asked them only one thing: that as soon as they found the Child, they would return to Jerusalem and tell him about it so that he too — as he said — might go and worship him. This, naturally, was not true, but the Magi could not have known that.

But God knew. He took care that an angel should warn them to return to their own country and their homes by a different route, without going back to Herod. And there was a warning for Joseph too.

As usual the Gospel narrative is so sparing of words that, at first sight, it gives no idea of the consternation he must have felt. It says: "After they had left, the angel of the Lord appeared to Joseph in a dream and said, 'Get up, take the Child and his mother with you, and escape into Egypt, and stay there till I tell you because Herod intends to search for the Child and do away with him'. So Joseph got up and taking the child and his mother with him, left that night for Egypt, where he stayed until Herod was dead. This was to fulfil what the Lord had spoken through the prophet: 'I called my son out of Egypt' " (Matt 2:13-15).

A Sign of the Cross

Once again the angel had come to Joseph in a dream. This time, however, he had not come to reveal a message of reassurance and joy, but to warn him of an imminent danger; not to relieve him of an almost intolerable burden, but to load one onto his shoulders. On the first occasion the angel's visit had banished all his anxiety; this second time, the disturbing nature of the news suddenly brought days of happiness to an end. It may be noticed that Joseph's reaction was the same on both occasions. As soon as he had been made aware of the mystery of the Incarnation, "Joseph awoke from sleep" says St Matthew, "and did as the angel of the Lord had bidden him" (Matt 1:24). St Matthew again, this second time, with reference to the menace of Herod, tells us that "Joseph got up and taking the child and his mother with him, left that night for Egypt" (Matt 2:14). He did *exactly what the angel had told him.*

The latest apparition was the sign of the cross upon a happy day, a day that had been perhaps too happy. It had indeed been a memorable one. The young Mother had contemplated with amazement how some great men had made a long journey, guided by God, in order to honour her little Child; she had seen how those important men had prostrated themselves to adore the son of her womb, and had offered him costly gifts. Joseph, discreetly in the background as always, had watched the scene with legitimate pride, perhaps thanking God for those marks of honour which, in some strange way, made up for the abandonment and poverty surrounding the birth. At the end of the day the Magi had taken their departure. Mary and he could draw breath and relax, their souls filled with serene joy, and overflowing with gratitude to God for the honour accorded to their humble state.

All at once, suddenly, without warning, without any preliminary indication at all or the faintest glimmer of a conjecture which might have prepared them, however inadequately, to face what was coming, this shattering revelation of an immediate and grave danger brought alarm and distress into a household where all had been peace and serenity until that moment. For the revelation was accompanied by a command which required action from them almost before they realised what was happening. Anybody who has had a similar experience will know what it is to be jolted from sleep by bad news or some awful message of catastrophe: such a person knows the feeling of depression and of being prey to nameless fears. Anyone who has been through this will have experienced the sudden confusion and the immobilising anxiety invariably accompanying such a state. The mind gropes in an impenetrable fog although it continues to register forebodings all too clearly. It is a state of mind characterised by a sensation of dismay, by a heaviness of heart and a feeling of unreality accompanied by the fearful certainty that what is happening is no dream; a simultaneous physical distress is not uncommon nor is a sort of imposed inertia, an inability to rise to the occasion promptly.

No doubt it was very hard. Perplexing, too, which

is even worse. However difficult a situation is, it may still be possible to see our way forward, especially if we know what is going on. But a defect of under-standing, an absence of information, in such cases always produces confusion. When for any reason we are unable to understand, when we fail to grasp clearly the true nature of a situation or an event because its meaning escapes us, then the state of interior confusion has such an inhibiting effect that it can prevent us from taking decisions. Not to know the why and wherefore of what has happened to us 'out of the blue' often causes such a degree of uncertainty and indecision that it sometimes becomes almost impossible for us to make up our mind how to act.

Perhaps this is why the angel told Joseph what he should do, as on that former occasion. This time, however, it was for a different motive. On the first occasion God's revelation brought about the resolu-tion of a terrible doubt which had rendered Joseph powerless to take a decision or to act. Enlightenment reached him after a long and painful mental struggle. In this instance, on the contrary, the matter in hand had to be expedited with despatch, so that the time that would otherwise have been given over to devis-ing a solution would not be wasted, since every second counted in the face of Herod's threat. It was not the time for questions, nor for wringing hands or giving way to useless grief.

The Gospel is expressive when it relates Joseph's reaction as the angel finishes communicating the command to him. "He rose up, therefore, while it was still night, and took the child and his mother with him" (Knox). Another version has it: "And he rose and took the child and his mother by night (and departed to Egypt) . . ." (RSV). In either case it is the same: there was no delay between his receipt of the warning and Joseph's starting to implement his instructions. Here we are shown another aspect of Joseph's character: In no way was he a person intimidated by events or hesitant in meeting life's challenges. "He faced up to problems, he dealt with difficult situations and showed responsibility and initiative in whatever he was asked to do" (Mgr Escrivá). This time Joseph did not take time to reflect. Reflection is good, and is normally necessary for the achieving of certainty. But the reflecting should come *before* taking a decision, when possible options are being pondered and studied. Once things become clear, however, once a decision has been made, pondering and temporising are over. It is no longer time for thinking things out, but for action. Reconsidering a decision taken after reasonable reflection (unless of course new factors come into play) is something very close to doubt and vacillation, both of which are paralysing in their effect. When it is someone else who, because of his position of authority or greater knowledge, has to undertake the preliminary reflection, and then decides on the most appropriate action for the adequate solution of a given·problem, all that remains to be discussed is the minimum of information required for the instructions to be understood, for the goal to be grasped, for one to obey and to act. It is no longer the time for pausing to ruminate on whether the ultimately chosen solution was the best possible one, or what the validity of its grounds can be, or if these grounds are sufficiently solid. "The best sort of obedience is this", says St John Chrysostom: "not to start searching around in quest of reasons for doing what we are asked to do, but simply to do it".

There is no doubt that had he been given to seeking the whys and wherefores of the situation he found himself in, Joseph could have raised for himself some very disturbing questions. Only a short time had elapsed since the circumcision. How could he forget that the Child had been given the name *Jesus*. And did not Jesus mean 'Saviour'? As the angel had said, he was to save his people. But how could he 'save his people' if he was powerless to thwart Herod's plot against him? Was such a precipitate retreat really necessary? Were there no other ways to avert the danger?

In general, when the moment arrives for them to obey, those whose trust in their own intelligence is excessive habitually raise such questions. They try to resist accepting what they do not perfectly understand, even when asked by someone who is in a position to know better. Joseph, on the other hand, had no hesitation in accepting advice. He was not the sort of man who goes through life convinced that he has little to learn from anyone else. But if he was, on the contrary, a man ready to accommodate himself to the plan of God, in no way does this make him a weak-minded individual. "His docility", writes Mgr Escrivá, "is not a passive submission to the course of events". To be 'docile' is not to be handicapped by a lack of energy or by a purely inert conformism. Rather is it the very opposite: it signifies a disposition to do, to be ready to make into a reality everything that presents itself as the will of God. Even less was Joseph one of those who see obedience simply as a surrendering of the will, as if nothing more is to be expected of them than is required of an inactive instrument. Like all of us, Joseph was capable of thinking. But that he was more than ordinarily capable he clearly demonstrated when he was wrestling with the incomprehensible fact of Mary's condition. He was capable of making decisions, even when they were personally hurtful and bound to be damaging to his own interests; we saw this when he was willing to get out of the way so as not to allow Our Lady to be compromised. What he did not have were those defects that frequently prevent people from doing what they ought to do — the kind of defects that incline many to adopt, promptly, courses of action leading to what pleases them, to take the easy way out, or perhaps to opt for what is least difficult.

Obstacles to Obedience

To obey is not easy. It raises all sorts of difficulties, the most harmful of which have their origin in pride. Indolence is another barrier to obedience, but, though crippling, it is not by any means the most insuperable obstacle. There is special malice in the lack of docility that springs from a mental attitude typical of intellectual pride. It is a kind of arrogance not uncommonly encountered in capable thinkers who, seeing things clearly — or so they maintain — reject automatically all authority and even all advice; people of great intelligence they make it their concern to dissuade from being convinced by the truth those who are at least attempting to consider the facts objectively. This is demonstrably the worst kind of prejudice and leads inevitably to irrationality. Maybe this is why it is often so difficult to persuade the intelligentsia that they are on the wrong tack — so sure are they of themselves that they are totally unable ever to yield their own judgement. It is of interest to note that not a few end by falling into the absurdity of pure voluntarism. They reject any possibility of submitting their thought processes to a reality which does not fit their own preconceived vision of things; they accept and hold stubbornly to a 'reality' created not by God but conceived by themselves. The clearest and best attested example of this kind of prejudice was shown by the Pharisees. They were apparently so unswerving in their esteem for the Law of Moses that not even when faced with the reality. of plain and palpable fact were they willing to change their minds and their attitude. How did they stand when confronted with the miracles of Jesus? "This man casts out devils", they proclaimed, "only through Beelzebub, the prince of the devils" (Matt 12:24). How did they react to the resurrection of Lazarus? "From that day", says the evangelist, "they resolved to kill him" (John 11:53).

Fortunately, we know that prejudice of this kind is not always irremediable; nor is it found in everyone. The absence of docility can stem not so much from ill-will as from a reluctance to accept what is beyond one's complete understanding, although the truth may have been enunciated by someone who speaks authoritatively and does know what he is talking about. Thus Zachary resisted believing in the angel's announcement when he was given to understand that his wife Elizabeth would bear a son, she being sterile and both of them being advanced in years. And it is not as if such good news was given to him in his dreams; it was while he was wide awake and in the course of fulfilling his duties in the temple.

We have then the fine example of a humble working man showing a mind both honestly open and more than commonly capable, adhering less to preconceived ideas than cleverer men and even than many good priests. For he "kept the commandments of God without wavering, even though the meaning of those commandments was sometimes obscure or their relation to the rest of the divine plan was hidden from him" (Mgr Escrivá). What comes from

God, and especially his inscrutable design for each one of us concerning our participation in the great mystery of the Redemption, has its own means of becoming known to man. But to be receptive to the divine Intelligence or to the communications of the Holy Spirit requires a little more than an agile mind or an alert comprehension. There are some things which are revealed only to little children (Luke 10:21), things that remain hidden from the wise and powerful: perhaps it is that children — and the humble, who resemble them — are capable of obeying with true docility. Without ingenious and marginal convoluted reflections, without the entanglement of rhetoric that paralyses the will but with, in abundance, that faculty which would enable them to align their will with the commandments of God, the humble of heart can live their part in the divine plan of salvation. Men can so easily become hopelessly enmeshed in the labyrinth of their thoughts that they trip over them. When they try to examine what they have been asked to fulfil, the results may not be very inspiring. For "a curious and useless investigation" (as John Paul II has called it) into the mysterious reasons for God's wanting something of men, only leads to a waste of precious time (which could prove fatal, as it might have done in Joseph's case) and, perhaps too, to the divine message's being stripped bare of its most profound meaning.

Obedience and Freedom

No one should feel that obedience — the natural or acquired disposition which allows man to respond immediately and with no apparent effort (and which is known as 'docility') — implies a loss or a limitation of one's own freedom. For us, Jesus made himself obedient even to death, and to death on a cross at that (Phil 2:8). But no one who has walked, or is walking, or will walk upon this earth has been, is, or will be more gloriously free than He. The highest freedom, the one true, authentic and unique freedom which can truly merit its name is the one that can enable us to say *yes* each time God addresses himself to us and says "Do you want to . . .? Will you . . .?" It is then when neither caprice nor internal pressure from passions, neither inducement from individuals nor allurements of tempting circumstances prevent us from saying *yes* to God's request; when no weakness or waywardness of the will carries us to where we ought not to go, it is then that a man is really and truly free.

Today, when the cry of "freedom!" resounds everywhere, those who are free and conscious of genuine freedom are, unfortunately, few in number. Submission to sin, resignation to the forces of evil and to the lower and worst instincts of human nature is ingenuously referred to as a splendid liberation from taboos and from repression. This capitulation in the face of evil would not be so bad if, at least, its proponents were to have the courage to call things by their proper names. But it is a capitulation to the extent that they decide to change the names of things so as to justify themselves; as if altering words could *ipso facto* change the nature of things and evil cease to be so by the simple expedient of calling it good. It is bad to disobey the precepts of God and to deny his Law. But worse it is — if worse is possible — to declare hypocritically that the Commandments of God have been 'superseded' and replaced by the commandments of man, for no greater reason than that of not being able to stomach a moral order whose existence points up the chaotic disorder of our lives.

As for the rest, in the life of the saintly family of Nazareth, "God, lover of men, mixed for them hardship with delight, a style he continues to use with all the saints. He gives neither consolations nor grievings continuously. But he interweaves one with the other in the life of the just. And this he did with Joseph" (St John Chrysostom).

We cannot enclose God within our narrow horizons and inside our limited capacity to know and understand. For to grasp infinity is impossible. In the last extreme, and given the comparative limitations of human reason (and in spite of its greatness) we will never completely come to fathom the mind of God, his ways or his intentions. They always transcend our capacities and our possibilities. Neither does a child have complete understanding of what his father does or commands. He confidently accepts and obeys. And this for us men is the only truly rational and intelligent attitude towards our Creator. It is also the only really effective one.

11

"Remain There . . ."

The same absence of unnecessary detail in the
Evangelists' accounts of episodes in the life of Jesus
is noticeable in the gospel references to Joseph. Only
the stark facts, the essentials with no literary embel-
lishments, reach us. This presents no obstacle if the
imagination — certainly at risk to a degree when it
reflects on revealed truths — tries with a measure of
common sense to understand and, above all, to
contemplate the narrative of the Gospel.

We will leave out of consideration whether, in
order to get to Egypt, the Holy Family used the
route parallel to the sea, that passed through Gaza
(the last town before entering the desert, where the
caravans would stock up with provisions and water);
or if they went through Hebron and the south of

Palestine, to get to Pelusa, this track also inevitably involving a desert crossing. The former journey was the less arduous although the road would scarcely have been thought an easy one. It was more popular with travellers, but was also, perhaps, the more dangerous in times of friction or persecution. The southern track was longer, more uncomfortable and perhaps safer. Both were exhausting. It could hardly have been a pleasant journey in any case, what with the difficulty of the road and the anxiety of having to escape. Another Joseph had made this same journey some centuries earlier, so it must have been full of memories for the exiles from Israel. His exile too had been providential, and it would be reassuring for them to recall that it had a happy outcome.

It was under the providence of God that the Magi, in adoring the Child, had given him a gift of gold along with frankincense and myrrh. Mary and Joseph were taken unaware by the urgent need for flight in the hours of darkness, with no time to ask anyone for directions or instructions or help. (The poor do not have at hand the resources to make long and unforeseen journeys or the wherewithal to stay abroad for indeterminate periods.) For them the gold of the Magi would be the guarantee that they would not be found lacking in the basic necessities, at least until the end of the journey, when they would be able to start afresh and make a living again. Perhaps among the few things they could carry, in addition to some clothes, would be Joseph's tools. A craftsman will be awkwardly placed if he does not have his instruments of work within reach. In cases of difficulty, they offer, if he has them handy, a certain security: he can always use them to make what the others need or will find useful. This would serve to keep the wolf from the door if times were bad.

The Stay in Egypt

Nor, of course, do we know exactly where they lived when they were in Egypt. The whole Mediterranean coastline was dotted with Jewish colonies, some more numerous and prosperous than others. In Egypt there were many such; they would be composed of settlers and of travellers like themselves, and of those small Jewish groups who, like Joseph and Mary and the Child, had sought refuge in Egypt from the vindictive fury of Herod. The Jewish communities of Heliopolis and Alexandria are known to have been particularly prosperous. It was probably in one of those cities with a colony of his compatriots that Joseph settled. To get along in a foreign country is not exactly easy without being able to speak the language or knowing a soul, and without relations of any kind. But even in these conditions it would not have been particularly difficult to find help if you were integrated say, into a community speaking the same tongue as yourself, with the same religion and race, the same culture and customs. A craftsman's skills are always in demand; there, in an unaccustomed environment among the outlandish idols of the Nile delta, in a notoriously 'liberal' society with extravagantly pagan customs, to find in one's own circle someone able and willing to do the small jobs that from time to time become necessary in every household, would have been, to a certain extent anyhow, a bit of good fortune for his neighbours. No doubt Joseph, after the first days had passed, would have found work, the pay for which would cater for their simplest requirements. They were, after all, poor; and the poor do not need much, for they are accustomed only to the bare essentials of life and will not miss the superfluities of luxury.

On the subject of the stay in Egypt, piety occasionally affords the imagination wings to take off and get really airborne. A good Dominican of the eighteenth century, Dom Pedro de Santa Maria y Ulloa, wrote a quaint and very devout book on contemplating the mysteries of the rosary. Its unusually extensive title already speaks eloquently: "The Rainbow of Peace, whose Bowstring is Meditation in order to pray the most Holy Rosary of Our Lady, and whose Quiver has five hundred and sixty Arrows of Consideration that Divine Love shoots into all Souls"! Here we are invited to contemplate, during the Holy Family's sojourn in Egypt, "our Queen sewing, spinning and embroidering, and Saint Joseph perspiring at his bench from morning till night . . . for the work of both would scarcely have been sufficient to pay the rent for the roof over their head" — such, or something not all that much unlike it, would have been the poverty they knew and the hardship involved in earning a living in a strange land.

Insecurity and Serenity

"Remain there till I tell you." Could there be anything more unsatisfactory than being in such a state of uncertainty? What the angel had given him to understand was that their stay in Egypt was to be a halt of undefined duration, which could equally well last months or years. It is uncomfortable not to know what to expect. How can a man put his heart into a job if he knows that at any moment he will have to move on and go elsewhere? When one is apprehensive about this, but does not know for sure, what serious enterprise can be undertaken if it will have to be left half done or even just barely begun?

It is unlikely that this kind of problem would cause

Joseph any real disquiet. Naturally, of course, the indefinite state to which he was committed by circumstances could have been as little to his liking as it would be for anybody else. But this unease would not affect him as deeply as it would do others. He was a simple man with a humble job. His thoughts were not of grandiose plans or of elaborate schemes to which his life would be 'dedicated' — the kind of works that are carried out while having an eye to posterity. Joseph was far too busily occupied to think of generations yet unborn or to create a *magnum opus*. Nonetheless his work was serious, just as serious as — or, who knows, maybe more serious than — the work of those who need every kind of preliminary security before commencing their task. Joseph was not one of those who never begin anything for fear of not finishing it. He did his work, whether in Egypt or in Nazareth, one day after another, one hour after the next. He did not look into the possibility of not completing any of his tasks through having to change his place of work, or simply, even through his death. Truly, he was not one for "easy solutions and little miracles, but a man of perseverance, effort and, when needed, ingenuity" (Mgr Escrivá). 'And is this not the way, the only way, for the vast majority of men — and for all who are poor — who have to get on with the business of living?

The future was most insecure. An old proverb says that the most used corner is the pleasantest, and that the unused one often fails to please. Arriving in Egypt meant starting anew, from scratch, as one might say. Everything familiar, all the possessions which until then had surrounded them in a warm and welcoming home, had been left behind, and to dwell on this would not make things any easier. He knew they would have to go back, and although in their new abode things would very quickly be the same as always, (for there are those who, when they reach a new place, create around them the most cheerful conditions in which to settle), it could not have been so easy for Joseph, or for Mary, for that matter, to make a house for all three of them on foreign soil. In any case, they could never have come to be completely settled — for this did not feature in God's plans. When, with their loins girt, their ancestors ate the paschal lamb, they had to be up on their feet, as if living their last hours standing up, ready to embark immediately on the return journey to their own country. We christians too ought to live in such a way on earth, for according to St Paul "we have an everlasting city, but not here" (Heb 13:14).

"Remain there until I tell you", the angel had told him. And there he was, undoubtedly uprooted and unsettled, but calm and serene though far from home, in the place given to him. It is precisely in this episode of his hurried flight from Herod and of his stay for some time in Egypt, that one can verify the penetrating observation made by Mgr Escrivá: "at no time does he seem to be frightened or shy of life. On the contrary, he knows how to face up to problems, to deal with difficult situations, to assume responsibility for and to take the initiative in whatever he was asked to do".

And so it was. The angel in each case had communicated to him only what was strictly necessary for him to know. The rest was left to the willing capability, good sense and experience of Joseph. To get up and go immediately, to set off for Egypt, to remain there until further commanded: this is what God wanted of him. The 'how', that is to say, everything else, was left to Joseph: what they had to take with them, the road to choose and to follow, the way of getting hold of what they would need en route, the place — once in Egypt — to settle in, suitable work once they were there and so on. Indeed, when a man thinks and has a sense of responsibility, it is unnecessary to ply him with instructions in minute detail. It is sufficient to tell him the goal and leave the rest to his initiative and discretion, knowing that he will do what he ought to do.

The journey from Bethlehem to Egypt was far from being like the gentle and idyllic picture so often portrayed. As described also by the writers of the apocryphal books, it was a tranquil adventure, and many were the miracles, the kindly highwaymen, and the fountains of fresh water shooting up and sprinkling the desert to quench the thirst of the fugitives. A forced flight could never have been as gentle as all that. The fear of being overtaken and discovered always accompanied those who fled, and made this journey for them a continuous nightmare. And Jerusalem was less than two hours away from Bethlehem. The flight was a rough one, six or seven days long. They would try as much as possible to look like the other travellers. For it is less than likely, despite all the lyrical landscapes, that never having moved out of Nazareth except to go to Jerusalem and Bethlehem, Joseph would risk travelling without the company of those who knew the way and had some experience of it. Looking over his shoulder for pursuit, avoiding embarrassing questions that could arouse suspicions about them or their reasons for being out on the road, Joseph would have his work cut out. It was no picnic.

And then they entered into Egypt, the land of the traditional enemy of the Hebrew people, already dominated by the Empire of Rome. The idols did not fall flat, prostrating themselves before the divinity of the Child who walked the terrain they had been dominating. They would fall, certainly, but for other reasons — through the preaching of the Cross and the coherence of the life and the faith professed by the first disciples of Christ. Egypt would be filled with penitents and hermits, with scholars and saints, and the idols would topple. This is a lesson for us christians who live today in an almost pagan world, because we too have a similar task — "not by doing anything spectacular, but by living with the naturalness of an ordinary Christian, sowing joy and peace around us. In this way we will topple the idols of misunderstanding, of injustice, of ignorance, and of those who claim to be self-sufficient and arrogantly turn their backs on God" (Mgr Escrivá, *Friends of God,* no. 105).

Cowardice and Prudence

And the flight . . . to take to one's heels is not always the resort of cowards. It can be, but is not necessarily so. It was not cowardice for Joseph to flee from Herod and his assassins to save the Child; not cowardice, but intelligent prudence. Fleeing from a danger one cannot avoid or overcome, and when there is no obligation to face it, is not cowardly, but very wise. Not to fly from dangers which threaten the life of the soul can be presumptuous temerity, above all when someone who knows how, and is able and ought to advise us, thoughtfully instructs us on what we should do. The pity is that we cannot always be as intelligent in such matters as Joseph, who obeyed the very moment he was told. For to be intelligent is to know one's limitations and to trust in one who is more knowledgeable. How often do we have rash confidence in ourselves, and do not heed the experience, wisdom and solicitude of the Church? How often do we do things badly and cause grave damage to ourselves as well as to others, and sometimes injuries which are perhaps scarcely visible but are hardly less real or less harmful for the Church, never mind our own souls?

There was, to all intents and purposes, nothing to keep Joseph in Egypt. But there he stayed the whole time for no reason other than the one supernatural indication he had been given. "Remain there. . ." And there he remained, patient, without a single gesture of distaste or weariness. He worked as if he would never have to leave there again. How important it is to know when to stay put, to remain in the place where one ought to be, concerned about one's own particular responsibility, without giving in to the subtle temptation against which *The Way* (no. 709) puts us on our guard: "Do you hear? Somewhere else, in another state, in another position, you would do so much good!" W. Farrell, an American author, wrote a few years ago: "the real tragedy is that most men live 'on the other side', traversing the ways of the world". Troubled and inconstant creatures, they are always wanting to be elsewhere, to be doing something different, being towed along by their own instability. Life is made even less satisfactory when our spiritual poverty, incapable of finding peace for us anywhere, is added to this anterior restlessness. Men who appear to be in perpetual motion, running away from God knows what, do not seem to be able to put down roots anywhere. It is not because they are on the go from this town to that, vacillating from one task to another (and this is no exaggeration), but because they never know how on Earth to remain calmly in the one spot, as if they could not bear to be there in their own company, fearful of being stuck in a rut. Impatient men, they are always under intense pressure, in search of an interior peace which they will never find. The trouble is that they seek it outside of themselves in 'entertainment' or in a variety of amusements so as not to have to face the fundamental questions of who they are and where they are heading.

Trials and Tribulations

St John Chrysostom, in one of his homilies commenting on the Gospel of St Matthew, considers with amazement the contrast between the power of God and His apparent indifference to the grievous troubles in which the Holy Family is constantly plunged. It is as if heaven, instead of being solicitously watchful of their needs, had left them at the mercy of the egotism and wickedness of men. And St John asks what meaning these hardships and financial stringencies, these deadly perils and menaces and that anxious attempt to escape could all have. He concludes that these vicissitudes present a memorable schooling for us: "Right from the beginning", he says, "one has to guard against temptations and snares". From the very beginning Jesus embraced the Cross. With Him, those who most loved Him and whom He most loved — the Virgin Mary and Saint Joseph — embraced it too. It is the legacy he has left us, the great sign with which death can be overcome. Thus St John Chrysostom again, who had no small opportunity himself to savour the truth of it, continues: "You, when you have worthily discharged some spiritual duty and then see yourself immersed in intolerable spiritual sufferings and dangers without number, let it not perturb you. . . . Suffer it all generously, realising that these afflictions come to all, and especially to those who live the most spiritual lives; and this is His legacy: temptations and trials there will be on all sides."

We ought never, then, to be alarmed by contradictions, by pain or by injustice; nor can we allow these humbling setbacks to make us lose our peace of mind. Everything has been foreseen. Some years ago, Cardinal Suhard referred thus to the Church: "How can one be surprised at her being constantly persecuted, often humiliated, and always suffering in some part of the world or other, if one reflects that her earthly progress renews the suffering life of the Redeemer?"

In spite of all this, one can nevertheless "remain there" because the grace of God is never lacking. When I shrink from where I ought to be, (for that is my place in the unfathomable and providential plans of God), then I run the risk of never finding where my place is, or even of never finding myself. And this is worse. I then become completely useless to my neighbour. Saint Joseph 'remained there', having left behind everything dear and familiar. His patient waiting, without complaint, without seeking any explanation (had the Angel's words not been "until I tell you"?) was further evidence of his stature as a man and as a saint.

12

He Feared Going There

Everything in the world comes to an end, and so did Joseph's stay in Egypt. "Remain there until I tell you", the angel had said. "But when Herod was dead, behold an angel of the Lord appeared to Joseph in Egypt in a dream, saying: Arise, and take the child and his mother, and return to the land of Israel. For those who sought the life of the child are dead. So he arose and took the child and his mother and came into the land of Israel" (Matt 2:19-21).

With this message, the provisional period which had begun some time earlier was brought to a close. There is no agreement on how short or long this period had been. There is a wide margin to choose from between writers. Some who are filled with more piety than knowledge of exegesis, like the previously quoted Pedro de Santamaria y Ulloa, perhaps with no better reason than quoting an older writer, indicate a period of seven years. Some modern authors, more careful in their calculation and with greater means and better methods, split hairs; others, erudite commentators yet again, like Maldonatus, give them just a few weeks.

Perhaps computing the period has been influenced by the few words of St Luke, who after describing the circumcision and presentation of Jesus in the Temple writes: "and after they had performed all things according to the law of the Lord, they returned to Galilee, to their town of Nazareth" (Luke 2:39). In general, one supposes that St Luke omits, between the presentation in the Temple and the return to Nazareth, the events St Matthew narrates, so that the return to Nazareth to which he refers is the return journey of the Holy Family from Egypt.

This is possible, although it is not the only possibility. There are even reasons to defend the supposition that it happened in a different way; that immediately after the presentation of Jesus in the temple they returned to Nazareth as St Luke says; from there they went once again to Bethlehem, setting up home in the town; here they met the Magi and it was from here that they left for Egypt.

This is the more plausible explanation and has in its favour some indicators not to be disregarded. The first of these is St Luke's text which explicitly presents their return to Nazareth "after they had performed all things" in the temple. In the second place, when referring to the return from Egypt, St Matthew allows a suspicion that Joseph's intention was to stay in Judæa. For it would not make sense if he had feared going there, when the place he had in mind from the beginning was Galilee. Then Archelaus reigning in Judæa would not concern him, as it was not to worry him later either. Moreover if this wasn't enough, why would the angel lead him towards Galilee if Joseph on his own was thinking of going there? Since the house he had abandoned on his flight to Egypt was in Bethlehem, there would be a logical explanation for Joseph to think in terms of returning to Judæa and not Galilee. Apart from its being difficult to explain his remaining in Bethlehem, "having performed everything", with nothing to do there when his home was in Nazareth, it would be equally disconcerting if Joseph had thought of going to Judæa on his return from Egypt. The journey to Nazareth which St Luke refers to after "having performed everything according to the law of the Lord", would have been in such a case to close up his home (if one can express it thus), collect his belongings and settle in Bethlehem, David's city being the most appropriate for the Messiah. There the Magi would be able to go, directed by Herod, to find the "newborn king of the Jews", just in the place indicated by Scripture.

In any case, to be able to determine approximately the period of their stay in Egypt, we would have to know precisely Jesus' date of birth. The opinion which allows him to spend just a few weeks in Egypt, based on the assumption that the adoration of the Magi took place after the circumcision and before the presentation in the temple, does not appear to have much to back it: little over a month to leave the stable, to settle into a house in Bethlehem, to receive the Magi, to go to Egypt, for Herod to die, to return to Bethlehem again, and to go to the temple to fulfil the law, appears to be too short a time for so many things. Moreover it seems that Herod died at least a year and a half after the birth of Jesus.

The Return from Egypt

Considering what has been established until now with a certain amount of confidence, one is led to conclude that between the birth of Jesus and the death of King Herod there was a period of between eighteen months and three years. Thus the stay in Egypt was no longer than two and a half years and no less than a year at least.

Whatever was Joseph's source for the news of Herod's death, it probably arrived with the caravan merchants or travellers. If Joseph found out in some such way by word of mouth, he did not let it influence his life immediately, although it did, perhaps, raise hopes that the end of his stay in a foreign land was near. The angel had not said "remain there until the death of Herod" but "until I tell you". The summons finally came, ordering him to be on his way to the "land of Israel", for those who had threatened the Child's life were no longer alive. Fr Pedro de Ulloa reminds us: "Ensure that you too do not return to your territory while the enemies of your soul live and rule there".

The road back looked little like the outward journey. Although the words with which the angel informed him of the end of the exile were similar — not to say virtually identical — to those he used to warn of the danger and order the flight to Egypt, there is nevertheless a difference. And the same applies to the words signifying Joseph's prompt response to the request. On the second journey there is not the anxious pressure of the first. They could perhaps take their time with their farewells, to collect their effects, and to make arrangements for the journey with one of the caravans that plied the route. Thus with a tranquil mind and joyful heart Joseph

would have set out with the Child and his Mother.
"With such holy company" — continues Pedro de
Ulloa — "you will surely return to your lost father-
land; do not travel without them." And this is excellent advice.

It would have been on the return journey that
Joseph learned about Archelaus reigning in Judæa,
almost certainly from conversations with those who
were going the other way. News and rumours would
spread in the talk around the fires lit for a meal and a
rest at the end of the day. The angel had simply said
that he should return "to the land of Israel" without
specifying a place. It appears — as has been said
earlier — that Joseph considered going to Bethlehem
in Judæa, but on realising that Archelaus had suc-
ceeded his father, "he was afraid to go there". He
wondered whether it would be better to go to
Samaria or Galilee — preferably the latter as there
was rivalry between the Samaritans and the Jews,
and also perhaps because Herod Antipas on whom
the administration of that province had fallen was a
man benevolently disposed towards the population
he governed. In contrast, Archelaus appeared to be
very much like his father Herod, distrustful and cruel
to his subjects. Such were the pleas and complaints
of the Jews that Rome was led to depose him nine
years later.

Once more the angel intervened. For the fourth
time — a fourth dream. It confirmed his decision not
to remain in Judæa but to return to the Galilee he
had left. There, in Nazareth, where he had got
married, where both he and Mary had received
God's call, he would settle again. This time it was for
good.

When one considers the life of Saint Joseph from
the time of his betrothal to Mary till his death, one

can perceive how accurate it is to say, as Mgr Escrivá has, that his was "a simple life, but not an easy one". He had, in effect, to begin his life again three times in barely three or four years — on moving to Bethlehem, in Egypt and once more on his return to Nazareth. The angel's advice was that they should return to his native land; they embarked on the journey with joy and hope, almost sure that all dangers had now subsided. But even now there was a trace of fear. For hearing that Archelaus ruled in Judæa — and this implied that his fame, his notoriety, was public while Herod was still alive — "he feared going there".

Joseph's Fears

The Gospel twice speaks of 'fear' with reference to Joseph. The first occasion is when the angel says to him, "Do not fear to take Mary as your wife", on his finding her pregnant. When he had doubts as to what he ought to do, he decided — as has been seen earlier — "to leave her discreetly". He feared taking her home to go through with the marriage. This fear has been attributed by the Fathers to causes which, although different and even contradictory, have a nexus which gives them a unity. According to some, Joseph feared having to shelter, with his conduct, a sin; it would also have meant going against what the law laid down. This view is now generally dismissed. According to others, he had some inkling, intuition or even certainty that there was some supernatural explanation. And considering himself unworthy to interfere in a mystery which exclusively concerned God and Mary, he feared taking her with him and decided to abandon her secretly. One commentator compares this with the later episode of the miraculous catch of fish when Peter throws himself at the feet of Jesus, saying: "Keep away from me Lord, for I am a sinner" (Luke 5:8).

In each of these two opinions, and apart from the specific reason each alludes to, the cause of the fear was none other than that of displeasing God. According to the first, he did not nor could not know by reason or natural intuition that his spouse had conceived by the Holy Spirit. And since the child Mary expected was not his, to carry on as if nothing had happened or as if everything were normal would be almost like making him an accomplice; concealing a situation of completely irregular conduct could not be pleasing to God. But according to an accepted view, he feared incurring displeasure by invading an environment into which he had not been invited. Thus Bernardine of Laredo says "it appears to him to be blameworthy imprudence to venture, of his own will, to accompany and to serve one whom he knew to be the mother of Him whom the seraphim are eager to adore"; if this were the case it would seem that the angel's explanation would have been superfluous. Which means that it was the fear of walking on sacred ground, knowing that one was not worthy of treading it. In both cases we may say we are dealing with a 'holy' fear, the fear of offending God, of saddening him, of the fear of doing something unworthy in the sight of God — a fear which has its origins in love.

But it was not this kind of fear that invaded him when he heard that Archelaus ruled in Judæa in place of his father Herod. "He feared going there" because settling in Judæa could be a danger for Jesus. This was not, then, a sacred fear, a fear of God which is a gift of the Holy Spirit and a fear related to the grandeur of the Divinity and to the world of the supernatural; nor was it a fear born out of love, or a fear which angers one in love. On the contrary, it was a very human fear, a fear for the danger Jesus could be in by being within the reach of a powerful man with his own resources and with no moral directive other than that of his own interest. This was a fear different from anything like the one that led him to take the Child and his Mother to Egypt. "Flee" the angel had told him. For as both St Cyprian and St Augustine say, to teach one to flee from the fury and malice of persecutors or from those who threaten with evil is neither a sin nor cowardice, but prudence. And Joseph was a prudent man, a man who did not expose his own to unnecessary dangers precisely because he was a man who feared God and was conscious of his responsibilities.

Two Types of Fear

These two types of fear are distinguished in Ulrich Becher's comedy *Mademoiselle Lowerzorn* as if in passing, but rather significantly: "In other times men felt a holy fear, the fear of God and his omnipotence. Today another fear predominates — man's fear of other men and the power of their secret armoury." This is a profane apprehension. It is not a fear of offending God or men, nor the dread of involuntarily endangering others. It is rather the fear that others who are stronger may cause us — or those we love — harm arbitrarily, in the name of any of the idols which occupy the place of the Divinity when faith is lacking in epochs or in men.

There are then, two types of fear — fear of God and fear of men — which produce different results. If fear of God — a principle of wisdom — does not totally eliminate profane terrors, it does help to overcome them with balance of mind. For he who fears God knows that His help is assured and that in the end victory is certain. And this hope is his strength. Strong reasons influenced St Justin when he rejected pagan philosophies and replaced them with Christianity despite the prejudices against Christian doctrine which the environments he frequented had inculcated in him. He was to observe the lack of fear in Christians facing death (death which was outside one's power to avoid), the serenity and peace and the lack of bitterness towards their executioners with which they were able to accept insults, calumny and bodily dangers: "I saw them" — he said — "so intrepid facing death and so impervious to the terror of things which men fear . . ." (*Apologia,* II, 12). The fear of offending God, a holy fear, brought them such strength that it seemed to immunize them against any other terror.

The same does not happen with profane fear, with its dread of men, which is not checked by the fear of God. Unfortunately it seems as though this is a characteristic of the present times. It is not the fear of God, the fear of offending him or displeasing him, which predominates. It is another fear, a fear that paralyses the mind or bewilders it into not thinking. Today such fear is universal. People fear a third world war with nuclear weapons. Men fear the knock on the door and the concentration camps of the Eastern countries. In the West they fear the kidnapper, the mugger and the terrorist. They know a fear which converts homes into prisons, with grilles, security locks and gates; people fear to go out after dark and in some places even during the day.

A kind of fear there is too that dominates the guilty and follows them wherever they go; this type of dark fear makes men hate and kill. For one of the causes of cruelty is fear. It is the fear that their culpability will be discovered and their dishonour exposed (conventional dishonour, that is, in the eyes of men); this kind of fear is peculiar to man, who can do everything except face the consequences of his own actions.

Perhaps this explains the regress of our time to the pre-Christian state. Clearly such reversal is not in the sphere of technical progress but is manifest in a declining respect for one's neighbour and in dishonest dealing among men. It has set back that love for others introduced into human relations by a general esteem for Christian doctrine. An age of faith drove out the egoism characteristic of the ancient world in which, nonetheless, neither exemplary men nor grains of the fundamentals of truth had been lacking. Perhaps this too made John Paul II exclaim in the homily during the Mass which officially inaugurated his pontificate: "Do not fear welcoming Christ and accepting his power! Do not fear! Open even more, open wide the gates to Christ! Do not be afraid!"

It seems as if the world, as if humanity itself, has taken fright at the thought of opening its doors to the heart of Christ and to the requirements of his doctrines. Men see their freedom diminished, put under pressure by the advertised attractions of this world's values, by, desires of the flesh, concupiscence of the eyes and the pride of life, says St John. Familiar with sin, they fear the inrush of grace and do not know by what mysterious process and chilling certainty they can be compared with those of whom Isaiah (6:9-10) speaks. He refers to those who will not hear with their own ears nor understand with their hearts, "it will be that they will not see with their eyes, hear with their ears, and understand with their hearts, lest they be converted and He give them health". What they are afraid of is conversion, of Christ's taking possession of their souls with his grace, a grace which would make them happy both here and now, beyond death even and for all eternity. Fear to reject sin, which even when it leaves them bitter and robs them of peace, agrees with their desires and momentarily provides some pleasure, for them the Dead Sea fruit still glows attractively, though they know well that it turns to ashes in the mouth. And fearful they are too that if they cut themselves loose from the despotic love which enslaves, it will turn on them and take its revenge by snatching away the wretched consolation with which it has bought their souls.

13

They Returned to Jerusalem

Only St Luke gives us the news of the episode in the Temple when Jesus, instead of returning to Nazareth with Joseph and Mary, remains behind in Jerusalem. The evangelist says: "Every year his parents went up to Jerusalem for the feast of the Passover. And when he was twelve years old, they went up for the feast as was the custom. After the feast, as they were returning, the boy Jesus stayed behind in Jerusalem without his parents knowing it. Supposing him to be with the caravan, they went a whole day's journey before seeking him among their kinsfolk and acquaintances. When they failed to find him they returned to Jerusalem searching for him" (Luke 2:41-45).

The Israelites came under the force of the Law's obligation from the age of twelve. Until then Jesus had not as yet been compelled to go up to Jerusalem for any of the three feasts on which it was mandatory to worship God with solemnity — the Passover, Pentecost and the Feast of Tabernacles. Although the Law did not oblige to go to the Temple those who lived more than a day's journey distant, at Passover-time Jews from all over Palestine gathered there.

The gospel indicates that Joseph went each year with his wife, although women were exempt from the obligation. *Ibant parentes eius per omnes annos in Jerusalem,* says the Vulgate: every year his parents went to Jerusalem. When he was twelve they took Jesus with them.

Nazareth is some seventy miles from Jerusalem by the most direct route. As Passover drew near, several families would join together to make the pilgrimage, keeping one another company and helping each other. They would break journey each evening after making fifteen or twenty miles; Jerusalem would be about four days away, and coming from as far upcountry as they did they would stay there for a whole week before making their way back to Galilee.

They would have begun the journey home, then, with Jesus remaining behind in Jerusalem without their knowledge. Given the circumstances this can be easily explained. During that week, Jerusalem had become accustomed to having a floating population much greater than usual. When, to begin the homeward journey, the caravans would re-form at the agreed terminal to begin the homeward journey, the scene would have been a confused one. The apparent chaos would be increased by people moving to and from the temple, or going about their own business in the bazaars. And then there were always the children. At the age of twelve they were not led by the hand. Both at the time of setting out and during the caravan journey their energetic mobility would allow them to be here, there and everywhere. Children are like that.

It does not seem strange then, that until the members of each family had gathered around for the evening meal, neither Mary nor Joseph would realise that Jesus was not there. They would think he was with some other group of neighbours. When they missed him, they would begin to search for him, spending the rest of the evening enquiring *inter cognatos et natos,* among kinsfolk and acquaintances. At first they would be expecting to find him at any moment, or at least to get some news from someone who had seen him. But there was nothing.

The night of the first day's journey north must have been dreadful. Early on the second day they retraced their steps and returned to Jerusalem, carrying on their search in whatever places he might possibly have been, asking whoever they felt might know anything at all. The second day passed, also fruitlessly. It was on the third day that they went to the Temple, not because they thought they would find him there; they would go there to pray and perhaps, to find consolation. There they found him.

The Parents' Anguish

The narrative is clear and straightforward and with its aid one can easily make progress without encountering major problems. But a simple narrative can be an account of an event that is far from being insignificant. It can relate a very serious misfortune or a long-drawn-out agony. But it can also describe a glorious deed. Ought we to consider ourselves dispensed from all reflection, which would help our resolve to deepen, only because the narrative seems brief to the point of being laconic and in itself not difficult to understand? The parable of the prodigal son, for example, is so direct and uncomplicated and in its development so clear even to the most unimaginative of readers that the question arises whether it could become an unremarkable teaching to be dismissed as if it were little more than an entertaining tale.

A certain amount of experience may be necessary (or at least, helpful) in order to understand and evaluate certain events; to try, if it is not always possible to relive them in a real way — for sometimes such a reconstruction is impracticable — at least to imagine oneself in one of those situations.

Neither Mary nor Joseph suspected that it was even possible for Jesus to have got lost. They themselves knew who he was. They had seen in him an obedient child, docile and considerate for the first twelve years of his life. There had not been the least trouble or sign of any bad example given by other children that could lead to danger or to any kind of reprehensible mischief. From this point of view they had absolute confidence in him; and very good reason they had for feeling this way.

When the moment arrived, then, he was missing. Time passed. He did not turn up. They began to scour through the crowds of travellers, asking one and then another. With no one able to help, concern turned to anguish. Only a mishap, a strange mischance of some sort, some unguessed-at wicked influence could have prevented Jesus from being where he ought (or where they thought he ought) to be. It is not difficult to imagine Joseph's grief on discovering his absence. He was the head of the family, the one whose only mission in life was to look after Jesus. What could have happened to him?

Although many thoughts must have rushed through his mind, this was one question he could not answer. It could only have been a very troubled night waiting anxiously for dawn, when they could retrace their steps back to Jerusalem. Once in the holy city, with sinking heart and heavy steps, they would begin a new search round all the houses of people they knew. They would call at every door, asking neighbours and passers-by, with increasing apprehension.

Perhaps worst of all was the apparent silence of God. She, the Virgin, was the Father's favourite daughter. He, Joseph, had been chosen to care for the two of them, and he too had experienced God's intervention in human affairs. Through the angel he had been forewarned of the danger Jesus would run in Bethlehem. He had been urged to flee to Egypt. On moving to Judæa once more he was told to settle in Nazareth, to avoid possible evils. How is it that on this occasion there was no one to advise him? How, after two days of crying out to heaven, of incessant searching and with ever-mounting anxiety for the child, could God remain deaf to his supplication and his suffering?

It is not easy to agree on this point with the opinions of Origen and Eutemius which are collected by Maldonatus in his *Commentaries*. They say of Mary and Joseph: "I do not believe that they suffered because they felt that the Child was lost or had perished. For it could not happen that Mary, knowing she had conceived through the work of the Holy Spirit, having heard the angel and seen the shepherds, and listened to the prophecies of Simeon, would now fear that the Child could be lost and be wandering around." What she feared we have no means of knowing. But if she had not lost him, what

could have caused all this distress? For it is the very
same Virgin Mary who says "Look, your father and
I, in anguish, have been searching for you".

It is much simpler to concur with Guillen de
Castro, who, imagining Our Lady in search of her
Son through all the alleyways of Jerusalem, hears her
exclaim: "Daughters of Jerusalem, have you seen
him? Have you come across a Child whom I have
lost, who is my Son, who is my all?"

As far as Joseph is concerned, it is very much in
keeping with his characteristic way of acting that he
would suffer in silence, trying to lessen the anxiety of
his spouse. God knew how deep his sorrow was. But
not even now, faced with this novel and incomprehensible event, does he utter the slightest complaint. Nor is his approach that of one who feels he
has been unjustly or unnecessarily subjected to trials
whose meaning or aims escape his understanding.
The words which St John Chrysostom applied to
King David, one of Joseph's ancestors, can fittingly
be applied to him too: "He accepted everything from
the Lord's hands without judgement, and with no
other rule than to obey and to follow closely the laws
which God had laid down."

On the third day he went to the temple, accompanied by Mary. All possibilities seemed to have
been exhausted, with no further searches left to be
carried out, no more inquiries to be made, and not
one remaining passer-by to be questioned. It seemed
as though, having followed every line of investigation, having covered all the places where he could
have been, there was nothing left to do but to admit
defeat and to go to the temple, the house of God,
there to implore for the lost Child once more.

It was at this point, when all human methods had
proved fruitless, that God once more solved their

problem, changing anguish to joy and unbearable
tension to peace.

Losing Christ Through Sin

When one thinks calmly and slowly about the text
of the gospel, it becomes clear that Jesus was not
'lost'. But if we think of Mary and Joseph, it was they
who had lost him. They would not have lost him had
either of them remained constantly at his side, if they
had not permitted themselves to become separated
from him. We cannot, of course, even think that the
disappearance of Jesus was the result of some fault
on the part of Mary or Joseph. No one had been
allowed to snatch Jesus from them. Nothing that had
happened to him was through any neglect of their
obligation to care for and attend to him. One may
say that Jesus left them briefly and temporarily to
look after his own business. But the two did not
know this, and suffered in consequence because they
did not now have him with them.

Our situation is different. "Look", writes the previously quoted Pedro de Santa Maria, "you do not
lose God. He attends to the dangers of this world,
where the enemies of your soul wander at will, so
that He may remove them from your path. He is
most diligent in looking after you." The inhabitation
of your soul in grace by the Blessed Trinity is a fact
— although it is a mystery well beyond our intellectual capacity to fathom. It is an unfortunate truth,
verifiable in a multitude of cases, that we can only
too easily lose this divine presence. In the case of
Saint Joseph, he did not lose Jesus; it was Jesus who
absented himself from his side.

With us it is otherwise because this never happens.
Jesus never abandons men. It is not he, as in this

episode in the temple, who withdraws himself. It is not He who separates himself from us. We men expel him from our side and — much worse — from our soul through mortal sin. It is we who depart from his company. Given the choice, we prefer others to him. Even in the most elementary processes of man's union with God, Christ takes the initiative. On the other hand, the process of separation is our initiative. He has never stopped being solicitous for our friendship, but he does not constrain us against our will to accept his own. But we are so fickle that it seems we will only admit him to our side if we feel deprived of the presence of others, and are ready to move away from him as soon as some enticing but created good seeks to enter our soul. No, it is not He who leaves us; but we who leave him. How could the same Jesus, who died on the Cross so that we might be always in his company, go away from us? He is constantly calling us with his grace, exerting on us his gentle attraction.

Unfortunately, it seems as though this is a matter of indifference to most people or, at least, to those who live in our own times. It is as though we prefer to run to whichever creature calls us rather than stay with him Who asked that we might learn from him because He was "meek and humble of heart" (Matt 11:29). It is as though we would rather serve mere creatures (who at times act like brutal and despotic slave-owners) than serve him Who assured us that his yoke was sweet and his burden light (Matt 11:30).

Falling in Love with Jesus

A statement in *The Way* explains both the grievous affliction of Joseph when he has lost Jesus, and his unrelenting effort to find him again. "What is the secret of your perseverance? Love. Fall in love and you will not leave *him*" (no. 999). Joseph loved Jesus deeply. That is why he suffered in his absence and sought him out untiringly until he found him. The truth is that today we christians (or those of us who call ourselves christians), present in our reactions a strong contrast to the attitude of this just man. It would seem that nowadays not many are grievously concerned by his absence from their lives. There are christians for whom the presence of Christ or his absence from their souls means practically nothing. They move easily from a state of grace to sin, and they feel neither sorrow nor affliction; there is certainly no feeling of anguish. They move carelessly and with equal facility from sin into grace, but fail to give the impression of men who have just returned from hell, or of having miraculously passed from death to a new life. One does not see in them the thankfulness, the joy, the peace and serenity of one who has to his vast relief rediscovered Jesus.

It happens because we are not in love; we are not exactly enamoured of him. For when we lose someone for whom we have great affection, and whom we truly love, the sorrow resulting from the loss is almost unbearable. But see how we men can lightly switch from having him to not having him, from losing him to returning to find him, with such cold indifference that there is no appreciable change in our outlook, in our mood or in our frame of mind. It is as if nothing has happened.

How difficult it is going to be for us to engage ourselves in an anguished search for a missing good, when we have not really appreciated that good! It can only result in profound sadness. It is truly dis-

tressing that we should repay with such icy indifference one who has lived so long among us and given
us his all. It is even worse that we despise and insult
him by giving him gifts that are little better than
worthless trinkets. At times, when we think about it,
we can get the impression that such lack of interest is
strangely like ignoring a lost child; not just any child
but our own. Such is our egoism, so concerned are
we with ourselves that there is not the faintest chance
that we will give him a thought.

The world hated Jesus (John 15:18) and it looks as
if it has in no way changed in its attitude to him. "He
came to his own, but his own people received him
not" (John 1:11). Joseph received him as eagerly and
readily as he received his spouse when the angel
asked him to, because She was already carrying Him
in her womb. He loved Jesus with all the intimate
love a father is capable of feeling for his child. He
suffered indescribably when he lost him. He sought
him unceasingly in every direction, in every nook
and cranny. He inquired of everyone who could
possibly have shed light on his disappearance, because he loved him dearly and life was unendurable
without him.

For those of us who profess belief in him in a world
that shows no sign of being willing to receive Christ,
Saint Joseph can give a very useful lesson. "Seek and
you shall find" (Luke 11:19). The words of Jesus
cannot fail. There is no doubt that if we sincerely
seek him we will end by finding him . . . provided
always that we look for him in the right place. For
this search we will approach a person who can guide
us (not someone who is going to lead us into an
empty wilderness). Joseph and Mary found him in
the Temple — the only temple where worship was

being rendered to the one true God. So too, the world will only find him in the one Church He founded, where He awaits us until the end of time, where the Sacrament of Confession permits us to discover anew the Child we had lost.

14

And Seeing Him They Marvelled

"After three days they found him in the Temple, sitting among the teachers of the Law, listening to them and asking them questions" (Luke 2:46).

This was the culmination of the search. They found him in the Temple, hearing the doctors' explanations and asking them further questions. He was seated among the masters who taught Scripture and the traditions of the people. (Where else could he have been? Origen says that "they did not find him where they sought him, among their kinsfolk; human relationships could not confine the Son of God. Nor could He have left his parents for anything less than the service of his Father".)

The Temple, we know, was a complex of buildings. Surrounding the sanctuary were a number of halls and chambers and courtyards set aside for various uses, all related to the worship of Yahweh and to the auxiliary services of the sacred cult. There, in one of those rooms or spaces, the rabbis would usually be found expounding to interested groups of auditors some point or other of holy Scripture. Their exposition would take the form of a kind of catechism, or of a more academic discourse depending on the age and degree of religious formation of their listeners. They expounded doctrine; they encouraged those who may have had doubts or sought clarification. At the same time they would ask their hearers questions to see if they had understood their teaching, allowing them then to introduce new topics or to delve still further into themes they had already begun.

Now his parents found Jesus "seated among the teachers", though not seated among them, obviously, just as one teacher more. This would be unthinkable with reference either to Jesus or to the rabbis, although the devotion (or perhaps the pious ineptitude) of some painters has portrayed Jesus as being on an equal footing with the masters of Israel, or even as giving them instruction. What the Gospel seems to say — and this is the general opinion — is that Jesus was with them, seated on the ground, on the customary mat or low stool, as the other members of the audience would be. And according to custom, he would hear the lessons or the explanations of the rabbis, ask questions, and reply when he himself was asked.

His questions and his answers would have had something unusually striking about them, for the Gospel tells us that everyone who heard him was astounded at "his understanding and his answers". It was then, while Jesus was replying, to the interested surprise of those listening, that Mary and Joseph suddenly arrived on the scene. "Et videntes admirati sunt" says the latin Vulgate; "and when they saw him, they were filled with wonder".

This is the second time the Gospel mentions such a state of mind in Mary and Joseph, although the words used here are slightly different. When Simeon praised God in the Temple, St Luke wrote, "his father and his mother were astonished at what was said about him". One may have been led to suppose that after the revelations Our Lady and Saint Joseph had experienced, and after the events following upon the birth of Jesus, they must have been virtually immunized against the effect of any surprises or marvels, and even more so against those events which were clearly out of the ordinary.

But Mary and Joseph were human. It was not only the words of Simeon that had surprised them. It was the whole event itself. No young couple, filled with legitimate pride and going to the Temple to present their first-born, would be expecting any other than the ritual gestures and words, and perhaps, some kindly expression of welcome. But to meet an old man, completely unknown to them, who, moving forward impetuously, took the child in his arms and, without any external sign to help him, recognised him as the Saviour of his people, who uttered words both unexpected and strangely knowledgeable about their zealously guarded mystery — this was not something that happened to everyone, nor even did it happen with moderate frequency. Small wonder they were astonished.

Now, on this second occasion, things were markedly different in several respects. Jesus had been forty days old at the Presentation. He had on that occasion been a passive participant. Joseph and Mary were surprised at the actions and the words of Simeon because they saw that he too must certainly have been permitted to share in the great mystery, and that he was filled with joy on seeing God's plans.

But now Jesus was twelve. Mary and Joseph were in anguish. What they saw seemed to have little to do with God, even if it was something commendable; instead, they saw Jesus in as odd a situation as they could ever have imagined. Nor, of course, were they surprised because they were seeing their son become a child prodigy, like one of those phenomenal children who appear from time to time, talented beyond their years. Such was not the case. Maldonatus notes that "the evangelist does not present him as a teacher, but as a disciple, when he says that he listened and asked questions, as befits a disciple". St Gregory is even more explicit in showing him here to be not a teacher but a student. He writes that Jesus was "found not teaching but asking". And he adds "In this example we learn that the feeble man ought not to risk teaching as if he were a master, for He, being a child, wished to be instructed by asking".

So Mary and Joseph marvelled at the whole scene. They saw the Child, barely twelve years old, very much at his ease, listening attentively, asking and answering questions. He showed neither diffidence nor conceit, acting with the total self-confidence of a child who is aware of where he is and what he is doing, almost as if his attendance at these classes on aspects of the Law were a matter of habit. His parents' admiration was, perhaps, not altogether free from a pure and legitimate pride at being honoured by the part he was taking. If those who heard him were also amazed at the intelligence of his replies, it was not because he was saying extraordinary things. Rather was it, as Maldonatus notes in his *Commentary,* because of "how well and how deeply he understood the questions put to him". "One has to realise", he adds, "that the masters would question him, as a student, on ever deeper matters, and that his replies would be far beyond anything they could expect from a boy of his age." Quite rightly did his parents marvel at seeing his aplomb and his approach which was both modest and confident, whenever he replied.

Although his audience admire him, at no stage however, does the episode go beyond the normal limits. Jesus would not attract so much attention to himself as to become the topic of conversation in Jerusalem. It is unlikely that someone would now take an interest in his abilities or begin to follow his tracks so see if a promised event would come true. The episode in the Temple was very significant, but it did not take away any of the anonymity of his hidden life. He was to continue unnoticed for many years yet. Those who were surprised by the brightness of his replies would quickly forget the incident; or, at some stage, perhaps months or years later, they would come to recall it in the course of some casual reminiscence in conversation.

The Privilege of the Humble

What is usual among ourselves, ordinary men, is that we marvel at the extraordinary. The rare occurrence standing out from everyday events tends to be one we have not grown accustomed to. We do not admire the sunrise every morning, for example. Nor does the dawn attract our attention. But even a hand-movement, or the alert, wondering expression on the face of a baby a few months old, delights us and strikes us as quite amazing. In the Temple it was not unusual to see children sitting around the feet of the rabbis, learning, listening, asking questions and offering their answers. From time to time a more gifted child would appear and its intelligence would show in the questions it would put and in the way it replied — nothing beyond the common and ordinary here.

In spite of this, these parents marvelled and admired. For them it was a revelation, although they ought to have been ready for this kind of surprise. But they could marvel precisely because they were capable of discovering marvellous things where the rest of us would perhaps find nothing but trivia. G.K. Chesterton once wrote of a Londoner who, after work, would rush off to a museum before it closed. There he would reflect on a highly coloured painting of a sunset. But it never occurred to this man to lean out of the window of his office and take a look at the splendid sunset skies God painted for him every day.

This is the privilege of the humble. It is to find something worth admiring in what is most commonplace and (apparently) devoid of interest, to wonder at simple things and qualities which others fail to notice. Mary and Joseph were, humanly speaking, only a poor young couple, neither of whom had studied deeply. They lived in a backwater of a village and did not count among their friends many intellectuals or members of the socially 'cultured' gentry. The humble are given more to listening than to speaking. The poor and untutored admire knowledge in others. They seldom raise their voices because they find it difficult to believe that what they have to say is worth listening to.

The gift of humility confers on men the capacity to admire others. Such is the self-knowledge of the humble man that for him to consider himself inferior to other men hardly requires any effort. It is almost like plain evidence lying constantly before his eyes.

It is the knowledge so admirably reflected in the perspicacity of those revealing words of St Paul: "What have you, that you did not receive?" (I Cor 4:7).

It is the clear awareness of the difference between what one has received and what one is able to give back in return that makes a person humble. Such virtue is unmistakeable. For he always considers himself indebted, without there ever being even the beginnings of conceit. He serves God with fear and is joyful with trembling. He keeps looking to Him to see whether what he is doing gratifies and satisfies Him. He wishes with all his heart to give Him satisfaction and at the same time, is convinced that whatever he may manage to do, it will always be very much less than what God deserves. In comparison with God's generosity, ours (when it exists) always seems more or less miserly. The humble man understands this to perfection.

But this capacity to admire, to be surprised or, as the Gospel says of Mary and Joseph, "to marvel" extends to the entire universe and to the least significant of its constituent parts. What humility does, is, in a certain sense, to turn him into a child. It continues to be a privilege and a gift, for the kingdom of God is for children. No one can enter who does not receive the gift of wonder as would a child (cf Mark 10:13-16).

The Capacity for Being Surprised

One trait the child and the humble man have in common is this ability to be surprised. A child is surprised by the flight of a bird, by the peal of a bell, by water flowing, by colours, by a burning light, by everything that is. It is constantly discovering marvels and being taken by surprise by them. Their life is a continuous feast. Simplicity and the spirit of ingenuousness which humility infuses into man gives him the same capacity that the child has for surprise. Man is surprised by the glorious spectacle of Creation, by trees and flowers, by the patchwork landscapes of spring and the golden drift of autumn leaves; glory speaks to him in the dark immensity of the night sky, with brilliant stars strung out like illuminated windows through any one of which he can lean out and catch a glimpse of paradise. He is intrigued by the fascination of the infinitely small, by the brain cells with their multiple connections and functions; or by the sounds and colours, the wind, fire or water. Everything is new, admirable and joyful for a child. So it is too for the one who has obtained from God the gift of humility. In this very same spirit of humility, capable of discovering a prodigious treasure in the most ordinary of things and of provoking a sense of newness in the most apparently banal, is created a source of youth and joy in those who possess it. It confirms the enrichenment of man when he contemplates the world created for his enjoyment.

But all is very different without this gift of humility. It is not because God has deprived him of anything, but because man, it seems, opts to despise it, and consequently neither esteems nor seeks it; he does not ask for it and does not obtain it. Here is the sad spectacle of men bored with everything. "These are old men, cynical and tired, weighed down by a firmament of decrepit stars, like sick souls whose failing eyesight is riveted on a clear sign crawling with flies" (W.Farrell). Their story is like that of many young people, prematurely aged by unhealthy experience, without enthusiasm, "to whom an exhausted world has been presented, and for which they are expected to become enthusiastic". How is it possible to enthuse them if what is on offer would hardly excite anyone who retains the last shred of discernment or sensitivity? For when there is no humility and the capacity to be surprised disappears, when man is incapable of wonder at anything at all because for him nothing is now remarkable; when one has lost one's vision and no longer perceives the light which illumines the work created by God as a splendid environment for man; it is then that weariness, boredom, and disillusionment set in, and one ends up losing the joy of living and even the meaning of life itself. It is then that man clutches onto anything to avoid feeling empty; it is then that he pours his excellent qualities and last reserves of energy on miniscule and fleeting objectives; it is then that he grasps wildly at ideologies, doctrines or ideals with the determination of a fanatic. He needs to take hold, even with anguish, of something, of anything, which will give him back sufficient interest to enable him to go on living.

The existence of evil is not a good enough reason for rejecting creation, nor is it reasonable to accuse God of having made the world imperfect. Even to say to his face that he had allowed the innocent to suffer and to protest that he does not prevent evil from gaining ground is not sufficient reason. Nor is there here even an argument. Rather is it simply a condemnation of the freedom of man. It is a wretched exhibition of the lack of a knowledge, accessible even to an unenlightened mind, on the part of those who should have known better. Whether later they have accepted or rejected this remains a decision which depends precisely on their freedom which they have condemned and denied.

Enjoying the Discovery of New Worlds

It is wonderful to find men as intelligent as St Thomas Aquinas being dazzled by the realisation that man is capable of knowledge. They are entranced by the power of human reason which allows men not only to know what is outside of themselves, but to be aware of themselves and to know themselves. "For the intellect to belong to the individual who possesses it, and for it to know through him, is almost too good to be true" writes E. Gilson commenting on the surprise shown by St Thomas. Nevertheless, what the powerful intellect of St Thomas found fascinating does not seem to attract the attention of many today. It is clear that he was such a humble man that he was continually learning from others. This humility of his enabled him to live in the continual pleasure of discovering glimmers of the truth even in the most mistaken of men.

It is moving, then, to contemplate Joseph and Mary, after twelve years with Him, being surprised by Jesus. He never stopped amazing them because they never stopped discovering His marvels.

But returning from many roads, disappointed and disillusioned, with aging souls and empty looks, we men of today seem as if we have rendered ourselves incapable of enjoying the discovery of new worlds. Having dominated — and almost destroyed — Nature, having tried so many things, having invented new ways of organising society, having failed in the effort to make the world a happier place (which is not so incomprehensible since men have had the pretension to rebuild it without reference to the Redeemer), the man of our day does not seem to have benefited much from all his ingenuity. He has lost both humility and the capacity to wonder, this prodigious faculty that lets him marvel at the works of God, that enables him to astonish himself with what he can do — thanks to the gifts God has pleased to shower on him.

Once again, these gifts have been revealed to the humble and the little. They have been kept hidden from the wise, from the powerful (which also means the self-sufficient), from those who believe so implicitly in themselves, in their talent, in their abilities, that they have become incapable of objective admiration. No longer can they see that their *I* is like a permanent obstacle in front of them; so dependent are they on themselves, and so confident of their powers, that they accept nothing except whatever conforms to their own ideas. It is very wearying and in direct contrast with the freshness and simplicity of men like Joseph and of women like Mary. Because of their humility they saw others as being great and worthy of admiration, while those who view men from the summit of their own arrogance see them as tiny, as insects on whom they can tread without fear of repercussion because of their insignificance.

But the little ones and others like them will become the first. Here, on earth, they have been made to be last. And they shall be exalted because here they were humble.

15

"Your Father and I . . ."

When Mary and Joseph found Jesus in the Temple and his Mother asked him: "Son, why have you treated us so?" and went on further to justify that question by speaking of the suffering his disappearance had caused them, she referred to Joseph as "father": "Behold, your father and I have been looking for you anxiously" (Luke 2:48). St Luke himself speaks of the time when Simeon "inspired by the Spirit, came into the temple . . . when the parents brought in the child Jesus" (Luke 2:28); "and his father and his mother marvelled at what was said about him" (Luke 2:33); "his parents went to Jerusalem every year at the feast of the Passover . . ." (Luke 2:41); "when his parents saw him there . . ." (Luke 2:48). Notice that he makes no attempt to give a precise definition of Joseph's relationship — no adjectives like "legal", "foster", "supposed", to draw the fine line. And really, once Mary's virginal conception by the work of the Holy Spirit has been clearly established, there is no need to go on pointing it out every time Joseph is mentioned in relation to Jesus.

But there is another reason. Joseph was, to all intents and purposes, Jesus' father. If the Register of Births had existed in those days, Joseph would have been listed as the father. The particular organisation and customs of the Jews were such — and this was clearly more than the work of human minds — that the legal father was the one who passed on to his children all of their rights. Merely biological fatherhood, then, is not the only sort there is. Our Lady acknowledged this when she spoke to Jesus of "your father and I".

When St Augustine wrote on Joseph's fatherhood, he put it like this: Jesus had been "born of a virgin without the husband's seed; he held both, however, as his parents. How do we prove this? By Mary's saying: *your father and I have been looking for you anxiously*". He continues: "She made more of conjugal hierarchy than of the dignity of her womb." (Sermon 51). For in effect man is the head (Eph 5:23). Why was it Our Lady then, and not Joseph, who spoke to Jesus in the temple? The reason for that lies in the special, unique bond that existed between Mother and Son. It was not really Joseph's place to call Jesus to account. His role was to work for, defend and look after Jesus and Mary. Was he, who had always been so silent even when he had the right to ask questions, now going to break the habit? This was the moment when what was to be done fell to Mary's competence, because she was more closely united to Jesus. And for this reason too, she would know what words to use, which tone to adopt. All of this does not alter the fact that it was to him as head of the family, and not to his wife, that God was transmitting, through an angel, what had to be done at each moment to protect the Child and its Mother.

What True Fatherhood Is

Jesus did not deny the title "father" which Mary had given to Joseph. For biological fatherhood is not the only kind of fatherhood there is. And, indeed, it is often inferior in degree to other kinds. Referring to children, Mgr Escrivá wrote in *The Way* (no. 779): "Many give them up for the sake of God's glory, and they have thousands of children of the spirit". Grace, infused in man at baptism, raises him to the supernatural order and makes him an adopted son of God and heir to his glory. This has no relation whatever to biology and yet God's fatherhood of the baptized is not only on a higher level than purely physical fatherhood, but it is more real and, of course, more lasting. "Our faith certainly tells us that Joseph was not a father according to the flesh, but this is not the only kind of fatherhood there is" (Mgr Escrivá).

We are making a mistake when, in trying to understand God's fatherhood of the baptized, we think first of human fatherhood and then transfer that image to God. We are mistaken because the truth of the matter is exactly the opposite. We cannot have a true idea of what human fatherhood is until we understand (insofar as our limited intelligence *can* understand) what God is to us as Father. He is the model. He is the one who sets the standard in this. St Paul has revealed to us that all fatherhood takes its title from Him — all true fatherhood, that is (cf Eph 3:14-15). Man's fatherhood, on the other hand, is an expedient God invented to bring new lives into the world. (And he could have found a thousand other ways.) He thus makes man and woman sharers in his creative power, cooperating with him in the creation of the body. He then places confidence in them to bring up that new being as befits its condition of a child of God, and to prepare it to inherit the glory of Heaven. And so St Augustine was able to write of Saint Joseph: "Whoever, therefore, would say 'He must not be called a father because he did not beget Jesus as fathers do' is making the essence of fatherhood reside in the libido and not in the affection of charity. He better fulfilled the fatherhood of the heart than ever anyone has the fatherhood of the flesh. . . There was no carnal knowledge between them, but Joseph was the husband of Mary by the unique bond of matrimony. From this we can see that Joseph can be called the father of Christ — the Holy Child being born of his own wife — with much more reason than if he had merely adopted Him."

A modern writer comments: "It is certainly true that the term *foster father* given to Joseph in relation to Jesus is too weak, even though it is better than calling him 'supposed' father or 'legal' father. Joseph does not look upon the son of his spouse, Mary, as an outsider he is adopting, but as the fruit of a virginity that is united to his own and which is the good proper to his marriage to Mary. Thus St Augustine is able to say that Joseph was truly a husband and father, and was such without loss of his virginity — rather, he was so by his virginity and by that of his spouse, Mary" (L. Cristiani).

Truly Paternal Care

It is not difficult to understand the force of this reasoning. We can think, for instance, of a man whose name is known to most people: Jean Jacques Rousseau. He it was who had the audacity to discourse and write on education — and have countless unproven and unprovable assertions on the subject both believed and acted upon — and yet have several children by Therese Levasseur and not be able to wash his hands of them quickly enough. He was their father insofar as he begot them. But he had nothing to do with them after that. For him they were unwanted nuisances. The most he ever felt for them was indifference. It would be irrelevant to wonder just how truly you can apply the term "father" to a man who gives his seed to fertilize a woman he does not know but who then conceives and gives birth to a child. And yet it is clear that someone who adopts a child he has not begotten but has taken from an orphanage or home, and then cares for him, educates him, works for him and pays out without question until the child becomes a man — it is clear that he is more of a father than the man who begets a child (perhaps without wanting to) and then has nothing more to do with it. A man is not a father just because he gets a woman pregnant. An exclusively biological concept of fatherhood belongs to the animal realm. Being a father is much more than that.

"The birth of Jesus in Bethlehem introduced this unique, exceptional family into the history of mankind. It was into this family that the Son of God came, grew up and was educated. He was born of the Virgin Mother, and entrusted to the paternal care of Joseph, the carpenter of Nazareth, who was Mary's husband in the eyes of Jewish law; in the eyes of the Holy Spirit he was the worthy spouse and truly paternal guardian of the maternal mystery of His Spouse" (Pope John Paul II). That "truly paternal care" is the expression of a father's love for his son. Joseph loved Jesus like a son: like a son received from his wife, although "not from human stock, nor from nature's will or man's" (John 1:13), but from the will of God. Bossuet addresses Jesus in one of his meditations with this allusion to Saint Joseph: "the holy man who adopted Thee, or rather, to whom Thou gavest Thyself as a son." The Son of God himself chose Joseph as a father.

Responsible Fatherhood

All these considerations ought to make us ask whether today we have not forgotten some basic truths that should be alive and fresh in the minds of all men, truths that should be especially present at the moment when men take on the responsibilities that marriage brings with it. From the very moment that marriage becomes the initial act which brings a new family into being, the man as well as the woman, (but especially the man, since he is the head), should be very much aware that marriage is a lot more than mere physiology. A pure physical fatherhood can be — an unfortunately often is — a very sad thing, above all for the children. And sometimes it can even be criminal. Avoiding children as though they were a misfortune, a hindrance or an embarrassment can hardly be called the paternal instinct. Nor would it be paternal, strictly speaking, just to put up with a child born of a mistake, a miscalculation, or in any case, not the fruit of a pure love that shows itself in the unconditional self-giving of the spouses.

Responsible fatherhood is not the term you can apply, either, to the type of man who works on columns of figures before deciding how many children he can allow himself to fit in with a certain standard of living. Nor to the kind of man who limits his family in obedience to the prophecies of doom meted out by some sociologist, or the planning policy of this or that government. Much less can you apply it to the type who carefully studies whether another child would jeopardise a holiday abroad, a second car, or quite simply, the peace and quiet of the home (so easily shattered by all the bother a baby can bring!).

Responsible fatherhood is something felt by a man who is truly a father, a father in essence (and not by accident, when the child is neither wanted nor looked for). Responsible fatherhood is not calculating, though it can be far-sighted. It is the mark of a man who does not block the source of life, whose link with his wife is not merely the 'libido', as St Augustine puts it, seeking the pleasure of union but avoiding its effects. He lets nature take it course and does not tamper with it, because he cannot go against what God has disposed. And if another child comes, well, he tries to get more money from his work, and he does not feel that it is a come-down either in his own eyes or in those of the people around him if he has to give up a few of the external signs (very real signs, at that) of his social standing in order to afford the new addition to the family. The amount some families fritter away on luxuries or on empty, useless forms of entertainment, would be more than enough to feed quite a few mouths. A child does not want very much, really: just care and affection.

Joseph performed his office as father by protecting Jesus from Herod and later by keeping him out of the possible danger that could have come from Archelaus. To do this, he left his homeland and stayed in a foreign land: he changed his plans as often as was necessary. He put his life at the service of Jesus' welfare.

He brought him up within the law of God, doing all that God commanded on his behalf. St Luke uses a very significant phrase when relating how Jesus was presented in the Temple. He says his parents took him up to the Temple "to do for him according to the custom of the Law" (Luke 2:27). The responsibility for this fell to Joseph as head of the family. He made sure he fulfilled whatever the Law prescribed for Jesus. In short, he did everything for Jesus that he, as a child, could not do for himself.

And he taught him a trade: his own trade, in fact. This is perhaps the aspect in which Joseph's influence is clearest in Jesus' upbringing. It is clear then that "in human life, Joseph was Jesus' master" as Mgr Escrivá says. And it is not unlikely that certain gestures, certain mannerisms, some ways of doing things, of handling certain carpenters' tools for example, would have come to Jesus through having seen them in Joseph for so many years.

A Father Protects His Child

We are now on the threshold of the third millennium of the Christian era, but there is still a lot we can learn from the lesson which Joseph gives us from two thousand years ago. First, the idea of self-denial for our children. To protect Jesus and to get him away from sure, lethal danger, Joseph left the city he had settled in, and took his family off into a foreign land to start all over again. The first duty of a father as head of the family, is clearly to protect them and keep them out of any danger that may threaten. People are more important than things. A wife and children are more important than social or economic status, and even than one's own job. Parents' concern for their children should lead them to foresee possible dangers, and to recognise that some moral dangers are more serious and have worse consequences than any of a physical nature. And here you cannot hope to get by with just the occasional once-over glance, or with having such an unshakeable trust in your children's goodness that you think they could never get up to anything more than an innocent prank, as though they had been innoculated against evil or confirmed in grace. On the other hand, of course, you cannot live on your nerves, imagining all sorts of dangers that could be dogging your children's footsteps, cross-examining them every day to find out what they have been doing, minute by minute, where they have been, who they were with . . . . until you wear them out or drive them to distraction.

No. It is a question of neither extreme — distrust or overconfidence — but of knowing your children, knowing their friends, taking an interest in their activities, listening to them, giving them advice little by little to help them learn to behave. Above all, it means loving them so much that you can detect the first symptoms of something going wrong and then nip the evil in the bud. It is especially good to pray and to entrust them to Our Lady. Let no man think, by the by, that this is the woman's job. Fathers have just as much responsibility as mothers. A man's duty as a father cannot be limited just to bringing in the money and stepping in with his authority now and again to settle some dispute where the mother has been worsted. Belief in that style of fatherhood has caused untold harm — and not only to the child.

One of a father's duties, and possibly the most

important one at that, is educating his children in the law of God. It may be that the great majority of fathers hang back in this respect of their obligation, either because they think that the mother or the school should do this job, or because they have no time even to think about it. It may also be because they think they have more important things to teach their children. Or, perhaps, they might even fight shy of it because they themselves do not take their duties towards God very seriously, so busy are they with other things. That is as may be. But the man who allows himself the luxury of being cool towards religion, who does not take much interest in whether his children practise their religion or not (perhaps he does not practise it himself), who thinks it is the woman's role to be religious (as if piety were some sort of physical defect in a man that should be hidden or at least disguised) . . . that man is not much of a father.

Joseph took good care to take the Child to the temple to do all the Law required. He made sure Jesus was circumcised at the proper time. He presented him in the temple and paid the ransom money. A man is not acting as a true father if he does not make sure his child is baptised without unnecessary delay, because otherwise he would be depriving him or her, arbitrarily, of an immense benefit. It is hardly worth mentioning here the stupidity of those who argue against baptism on the silly pretext of respecting the child's freedom and waiting until he asks for it himself, or until he is old enough to decide. G.K. Chesterton turned his irony loose on the attitude of a young mother he overheard saying: "I don't want to teach my child any religion. I don't want to influence him. I'd like him to choose for himself when he grows up." Where, asked he, is the logic of applying that principle *only* to religion and not to anything else? This is not respecting freedom, but abusing common sense. There is such an inconsistency of thought here that only dire ignorance could possibly account for it.

A man is not acting as a good father if he is not well acquainted with the school and the men and women to whom he is entrusting his children's education. For, in the wrong environment, children can be led astray in a very short time — to the point of no return. A father should teach his children by example, because if a father does not lead, the children will not follow. He should teach them to fulfil all that God commands by taking them to Confession and to Mass. He should instruct them in the Commandments of God and of the Church, explaining their meaning in such a way that, at the same time as they grow in age, they also grow in wisdom — and not just in worldly knowledge. Obviously, this means that the father needs to know these things himself. And he has to make time to spend with his children. But both these things are easy where there is a will. True interest in one's children will always find a way around any obstacles.

Naturally, though, there comes a time when a father's authority has to give way to a child's free will. Then the child may or may not continue in the practice of those good things he ought to do in relation to God, and to which he has been brought up. But now it is his affair. The father will already have done his duty to his children in the eyes of God. If, now, when they are exercising a choice the children opt for the wrong thing — for that mysterious reason which defies all rational understanding — well, that is sad. It will doubtless upset the parents and cause them pain, but that is the risk of freedom.

A Father Gives His Child a Livelihood

And then teaching a trade. It is another of a father's duties to put his children on the way to being able to make a living. And here we need to inject a new element of criterion. Parents generally tend to choose a profession for their children that is, objectively speaking, the very best. And that is only natural. What is objectively the best, however, may prove disastrous for certain individuals. Objectively speaking, and in the eyes of all the world, you would say that being a solicitor with a good private practice is a much better prospect than being a mechanic. But if a lad likes mechanics and has the talents and skill that the job demands, then forcing him to go on for higher studies to read law at university will probably ruin his entire life. Who will say that being a second-rate solicitor with a mediocre practice is better than being a good mechanic?

You have to keep a look out for your children's talents, their hobbies, the kind of work they like. Forcing what can truly be called a professional vocation is not only unjust, but could also be condemning a child to a wretched life. To spend a lifetime doing something you do not like is a very hard thing to put up with. And parents have a duty to be courageous enough to relinquish their dreams for their children so that the children can have, and fulfil, their own dreams. There is no point in fighting for what would be a lost cause. Higher education is a wonderful thing, but it would be a waste of money to pay for a child to go on and on when he or she shows no interest at all in study and is getting poor results. Apart from that, it is doing scant service to the child itself, letting him get used to doing little or nothing at an age when he ought to be doing something, or at least training to do something. And it usually does not work out for the best, even though the father may find it more comfortable, to keep putting off difficult decisions.

No. Being a father is not easy. Joseph made a good job of it because he gave himself whole-heartedly to his mission. He knew enough to bring the child up in the Law and to teach him a trade. His union with God did the rest. He was not brilliant. He was not very learned in any branch of knowledge. And he did not make his name as an educator. But men can learn much from him and pick up some of the things needed to perform well in the difficult job that fatherhood confers on them.

16

They Did Not Understand His Reply

After the anxious days Mary and Joseph had spent searching for Jesus, their first emotion on finding him in the Temple was, without doubt, one of immense relief. The weight that had oppressed their hearts now vanished like mist with the sun's rays. It left in its place that particular state of internal relaxation which one feels when tension caused by an argument ceases.

On seeing Jesus, they — Mary and Joseph — reacted instinctively. They had found him, and all anguish ceased. The cause which had provoked their worry had disappeared. This was only in the very first moment, as a natural and spontaneous, almost subconscious reaction. It was like the *feeling* one has when a physical pain diminishes or goes away. But then, without losing their recently acquired serenity, and precisely because of it, another emotion was growing. It was greater in Our Lady, but was also present in Saint Joseph.

The Roles of Joseph and Mary

What was it they saw on reaching the temple? Jesus was seated, listening, probably with other children, and asking questions of the learned. Mary and Joseph felt cheered and they marvelled. But there was more. Only later, and perhaps by contrast, after the initial reaction of relief and admiration, were they able to observe this. For the serenity of Jesus contrasted itself with the affliction they had suffered during those days. The composure of Jesus in the nave of the temple, listening to the rabbis as if it were his habit, was in marked contrast with their incessant activity in searching for him everywhere. Their disquiet, concern, suffering and even, probably, their physical distress compares strikingly with the calmness he showed. They had missed him so much that it had produced sorrow; but he seems not to have missed them. They suffered for him; but it seems that he did not suffer for them. All this was disconcerting and inexplicable, for until that moment there had always been understanding and harmony. The three had always vibrated in unison, with full confidence and without misunderstandings. Now it seems they did not share the same things. It seems as if Jesus had not realised the anxiety and concern he had caused his parents by working on his own and remaining behind in Jerusalem without letting them know. This is strange, for never before had he acted with such lack of attention towards them. Mary and Joseph were heartbroken. But it seems as if Jesus was not.

This event probably caused Joseph and Our Lady each to suffer in a different kind of way. Our Lady was more united to Jesus than was Joseph. Her union with him had an intenseness and special aspects which Joseph could not have. Reading between the lines of the gospel narrative, it seems that Joseph, in his turn, was aware of this. Although he was head of the family, it was Mary who addressed Jesus and not Joseph. This indicates that he knew that beyond a certain limit there was an area in which he would never be able to work with the same confidence and naturalness with which Our Lady could. It was she, then, the Mother, who questioned Jesus: "Son, why have you treated us so? Behold, your father and I have been looking for you anxiously."

He was a child of twelve. And a twelve year old cannot work independently of his parents. He could not tackle on his own matters which affected others, as if he himself did not depend on anyone. There was, in a sense, a second sorrow, distinct but no less real. It was the realisation that Jesus had not been lost; he had deliberately stayed behind in Jerusalem, without having sought their permission, without even letting them know. This hurt more, for it would seem that he lacked confidence in them. It seemed as if he feared they might have opposed his plans. If this was not the case what other explanation could there be? What would it have cost him to explain that he wanted to stay in the Temple with the rabbis to listen to their explanation of the scriptures?

And so we can explain both the sorrowful complaint of Our Lady and the attitude of Saint Joseph. He refrained from taking the initiative, for he knew less and he was also aware of his role. It is a very typical trait in this just man that he does not step beyond the limits within which he may act. And at the same time he shows great sensitivity and consideration, not ever interfering in the intimate relationship between Jesus and Mary. He was not the one to ask Jesus for an explanation.

In this part of the episode, Joseph was once again a spectator, but by no means a stranger. In him there was not the indifference or the disinterest of the simply curious. He was more than interested; he was involved. Nothing that referred to Jesus or his Mother could be alien to him. His life was committed to and indissolubly united to theirs. Nonetheless, he did not intervene. In this sense he can be called a spectator. Perhaps because of what he was, he could not but be carried away by those natural and instinctive reactions which arise so spontaneously that they almost always lead to regret.

The Enigmatic Reply

"How is it that you sought me? Did you not know that I must be in my Father's house?" (Luke 2:49). Jesus' reply was disconcerting, even for us. Disconcerting, in spite of the many explanations exegetes have left us. Although it was a significant reply, it was not one lacking in respect. For the first time Jesus shows someone outside who he was: the Redeemer sent by the Father to save men, and not dependent on any creature. This independence is clearer in what perhaps may be considered as his first action as the Only Begotten of the Father as distinct from the son of the Virgin Mary. His reply was as if to point out to Joseph and Mary the limits within which henceforth they were to exercise their authority. It was like a reminder of what they already knew: that he had come, above all, to carry out the work entrusted to him. Being who He was, his obedience to the Father was not subject to the authority of creatures, even when they were as excellent as Mary and Joseph. For although their role, developing in unison with the Redemption, was important, it did not give them the right to know those details of God's plans or decisions which He did not choose to communicate to them. Nor even less did it give them the right to approve them.

St Luke makes a significant comment on the reaction of Our Lady and Joseph as soon as Jesus answered. "But they did not understand his reply", he says. This lack of understanding was not, however, a problem for them. Ronald Knox, with his usual incisiveness, comments that not understanding Jesus' reply to Our Lady did not matter to them. It was sufficient for them to know that an explanation was available for that anomalous event; to know that there had been a reply although they did not understand it. And really here too, with their behaviour, they have taught us another splendid lesson.

Exegetes and commentators on the Gospel each have their own way of interpreting Jesus' words. Maldonatus, for example, is not satisfied that these words were simply not understood. "They had indeed understood the meaning of the words calling God his father, whose business he had to look after. For they could not be unaware of this after the scenes with the angels, with the shepherds, with the Magi and with Simeon and Anna. But the mystery enclosed in these words is what they did not understand. They did know what his Father's business referred to — first to teach and then to die for them". Others explain that his parents did not comprehend the reply of Jesus in all its depth and all its extension.

"But they did not understand him." Perhaps looking at an analogous passage of the gospel may help us deepen a little our understanding of the meaning of this expression. What is more important is that from Mary and Joseph's behaviour we may be able to deduce a lesson for our own lives. When Jesus began to reveal the mystery of the Redemption to the disciples, saying it was convenient that the Son of Man should be given up to the gentiles, scourged and crucified, and that he would rise again on the third day, the evangelist comments that they did not understand him. They evidently understood each and every word, and they understood all the words put together — the sentence. But they could not understand what he wanted to say to them. They missed *the meaning* of what he said.

This is not strange. Jesus was twelve. He had not spoken to them like that before. These were the words of an adult, not of a child. They were said with authority, with the awareness of their content and of Who he was. They were not used to the way Jesus had spoken to them on this occasion. It was a surprise. Perhaps what they expected — what we all surely would expect — after the gentle and sorrowful complaint of Our Lady, was some expression of regret for what they had suffered on his account, and for his not having realised this. But he did not make the reply which, according to our human way of seeing things, we feel ought to have been made. He made another very different and totally unexpected one.

For them it must have come like a flash of lightning, as a shock. They were accustomed to the placid serenity of those pleasant years at Nazareth. Jesus had grown up without showing any sign of his origin or of any ability out of the ordinary and above the natural. It was also a reminder of who he was — the Only Begotten Son of the Father, God Himself.

Mary and Joseph could see that something had happened. Something beyond their comprehension and beyond their authority had begun to develop.

They were humble, and not to understand Jesus' reply did not matter to them. It was enough for them, as it is with children, to know there was an answer which they did not understand.

And this ought to be sufficient for us too. It would be, if we were humble. But we are not. So, at times, we are troubled and irritated. We lose our peace and formulate distressing questions which then get entangled in our mind, complicating a straightforward view of the faith. There are moments in the life of every person when pain, contradiction, injustice or misfortune weigh heavily on the soul. And one feels one's inability to tackle the unjust danger coming to us from the outside. It seems as if one is to witness evil triumph. The man who tries to live honourably seems crushed and trampled upon by those quicker and sharper than he. He is then called naive for not using the 'effective' means to triumph and success. Or one seems flattened by all sorts of pressures which then have their repercussions on those one loves and is responsible for. It is in these moments that temptations surge in on good men and women, just when the mettle of each one is being discovered.

The Problem of Evil

Man has no easy answer to some of the problems that arise in life and some of the questions that are raised. There are, of course, easy answers which, although they are true, do not satisfy. The existence of evil ('existence' being only a manner of speaking here, for evil is the absence of good, like a vacuum which should be filled) is an example. Why does God permit it when he could prevent it? Why is the suffering of the innocent accepted? Yes, there are reasons. The theologians give reasons, and at an intellectual level their reasoning is faultless, but. . . . Pure reason is not enough for the majority of people. They do not understand it, perhaps, because man is not only an intellect. And often the intellect does not manage to overrule what the heart feels. Either that, or its own limitations prevent it from getting to the bottom of the answer.

But is it necessary to understand something to be able to accept it? Is it necessary for everything to be so small that it can be accommodated by our very limited intelligence? The problem of evil and of the suffering of the just and innocent was posed long ago. In the Book of Job it is analysed in unsurpassed depth with great beauty. There is Job, patient and grieving under the assault of unprecedented calamities. His friends Eliphaz, Bildad and Zophar have "sat with him on the ground for seven days and seven nights" without saying a word. "Seeing how great was his sorrow" (Job 2:13) they speak to him in turns trying to persuade him to recognise his sin. (For if God is punishing him, he has certainly committed sin.) He would then be forgiven, they maintain, and the punishment be suspended. And thus it continues, until God, speaking to Job, makes them see their limitations. "Gird up your loins like a man. I will question you and you shall declare to me. Where were you when I laid the foundation of the earth? Tell me, if you have understanding." And the questions keep flowing, with no reply, "Who shut in the sea with doors? Have you, in your life, commanded the morning and caused the dawn to know its place? Where is the way to the dwelling of light? Declare if you know this? Where is the place of darkness? Have you been to the storehouses of the snow? What is the way to the place where the mists are distributed? Who has opened a way for the thunderbolt? Can you send forth lightnings that they may go and say to you 'Here we are'?"

The Certainty of Faith

There are so many things we ignore, so many things that we do not know about without feeling disquiet, without being irritated or sceptical that a few more should not concern us. The gnostics of old wanted to understand in order to believe. But they put the question the wrong way round. For only he who believes can attain understanding. Furthermore, mystery exists. It is real even when we do not understand it. Someone has said that "the essence of many questions lies precisely in that no adequate human answer can be given". With our limited intelligence we have to admit that there will be answers which we have to accept for the sole reason that He has given them to us. It isn't necessary to understand before accepting; often it is enough simply to love.

Today, perhaps, the world — both men and institutions — is drifting so badly, with everything in turmoil and lacking direction precisely because human reason will not admit anything it does not understand. And what it understands is very little. Rather than admit a moral law which does not depend on ourselves, a human nature fallen and then redeemed, or a reply we are not capable of understanding, we prefer to create a system and then give a "rational" explanation of man and the world. In philosophical terms we would call it 'rationalist'. But all this is to no purpose.

Just as the heavens are separated from the earth,

and the east from the west, so are the ways of God different from our own. How are we going to understand the designs of God? For him it is enough that we trust in his love for us, as a child trusts the love of his parents. Children ask questions; they receive replies; they do not understand, but they go away quite satisfied, because they have received a reply to their question. They do not understand. But what does that matter? Even in human affairs it is impossible to live under the pretence of understanding everything.

"They did not understand his reply", but they did not go further because it was enough that Jesus replied. They knew he had a reason, although they they could not fathom it. It was sufficient for them. It ought to suffice us too if, like them, we know with the certainty of faith that Jesus is God. Consequently everything he says is certainly true, for He is Truth itself.

17

He was Subject to Them

After the Temple episode, St Luke buries eighteen years in barely three lines. He says "he went down with them on their journey to Nazareth, and lived there subject to them, while his mother kept in her heart the memory of all of this. And so Jesus advanced in wisdom with the years, and in favour both with God and with men" (Luke 2:51, 52). Joseph is not mentioned explicitly in the text. But he is included in the expressions "he went down with *them*" and "subject to *them*". Jesus went with Mary and Joseph; he was subject to Mary and Joseph.

Of these eighteen years, it is not known for how long he was subject to Joseph. For although it grieves us, there is no way of discovering when the holy patriarch died. There is a general consensus that it was before Jesus began his public life — a consensus based on very reasonable observations and on arguments, which are difficult to rebut. But for whatever period Joseph lived, what is certain is that from the time of his flight into Egypt until he left this earth, his mission being accomplished, he is only mentioned when the account of the journey to Jerusalem for the Passover is being narrated. He is not referred to again except indirectly.

This does not imply that his life from that moment on, or his mission beside Jesus and Mary must have lost importance, but merely that nothing happened to him that was out of the ordinary. Nothing stood out, over and above the common and unexceptional, nothing in particular which would have to have been recorded.

When the Gospel says Jesus was "subject to them", what is meant above all, or principally, is that Jesus obeyed them. He was subject to the authority of Joseph and Mary. And with Joseph being the head of the family Jesus was subject to his authority; and it was not a purely theoretical and formal authority, but a real, exercised authority. It could not be said of Jesus that he obeyed if there was no one to obey. And this always implies that there is someone in command.

There are also extra-biblical texts which clarify the obligations (or at least, some of them) which parents in Israel had towards their children. "Duties of a father to his son: to circumcise him, to redeem him, to instruct him in the Torah and in a trade, to find him a wife". The two areas of instruction here, that of the law of God and that of a trade, call for a teacher and a disciple; someone who knows and teaches; and someone who is ignorant and is taught. Until he was twelve Jesus could not come of age under the law, which thereafter empowered men — and even obliged them — to visit the Temple at the Passover.

Meanwhile Jesus obeyed his parents, as all children do, and evidently was subject to them. Why then does St Luke, or rather the Holy Spirit through St Luke, feel it opportune to say that "he was subject to them" on his return to Nazareth after the episode in the Temple? Why does he choose to relate it precisely at this moment, and not refer to the previous years, before adolescence, when he would have been so obviously subject to them?

A Turning Point

It is beyond doubt that Joseph had authority and exercised it. One cannot educate without pointing out what has to be done, what is good and what is evil, and the way one has to act. Jesus, like all children (and there is not the slightest indication in Revelation to say otherwise), learnt to walk and to speak, was taught to recognise objects, how to do things, to behave. Both Mary and Joseph taught him and had influence over his human personality. We do not know if before the event at the temple, with those mistakes which children can make while they are learning, Jesus had to be corrected. Mary and Joseph would have done so. In any case, there was something in that episode in the temple which catches our attention with the apparently unimportant phrase "he was subject to them". It distinguishes in some way the subjection of Jesus after the episode from his subjection before it.

On the occasion of the journey to Jerusalem for the Passover, for the first time Jesus had adopted a different attitude in the temple. Something had happened. From then on things would never be the same. Jesus continued being subject, Joseph retained authority in the family, but both Jesus' obedience and Joseph's authority would have taken on a different shade. Jesus had explicitly withdrawn part of his life from family authority, making plain his independence when a matter related to the "things of my father". For a brief moment and with great clarity he had been shown to them as Messiah and from then on, life could not go on as if nothing had happened. To mention explicitly after this that "he was subject to them" appears to indicate that Jesus, in full conscience, obeyed not only voluntarily everything in Joseph and Mary's competence (this he had already been doing previously) but now he obeyed with greater deliberation, with greater freedom, as if accentuating the importance of unity in the family, in which there ought always to be a head and an authority.

There was little left for Joseph to teach Jesus — if anything at all — with reference to the Law, but there would be much in the trade. Joseph kept to the limits within which he could exercise authority, and Jesus continued to be subject always. But we cannot only think in terms of commands and orders and a servile obedience. To exercise authority in this case would have been perfectly in keeping with Jesus' disposition and Joseph's knowledge of who Jesus was. And, above all, because love gave such unity to the three, a slight suggestion, a word, a look, would be enough to ensure perfect understanding and compliance.

If God had wished his Son to abide — in human terms — by the order He had established by being born, growing up and being educated in the midst of a family, it is evident that he also wished for everything which such a scheme entailed. God wished that Jesus live as subject, obeying authority in the family; he would allow himself to be educated and would

learn a trade. And so he had to be subject to someone who would have the authority to rule, the obligation to educate and be willing to teach whatever was
appropriate. This, then, was the role of Joseph, and
his part in what we may consider to be the human
progress and development of Jesus.

The statement "he was subject to them" expresses, on the one hand, as much the fulfilment
of the Father's desire that his Only Begotten Son
be subject, as the will of Jesus to remain subject to
those whom God had chosen to govern the family of
which he formed a part. On the other hand, as much
the obligation of Joseph to educate and teach Jesus
as it would have been for Jesus to be docile and learn
what, humanly, he needed to develop in the environment in which he would live.

Generally, commentators on the Gospel — and
the Fathers, of course — naturally concentrate on
the example Jesus gives. Thus Maldonatus says (in
line with Origen and St Ambrose, St Bede and
others), that it seems as if the evangelist had placed
special emphasis in observing that he was subject to
them. "One is not to think that Christ had been
emancipated and that in dedicating himself to his
Father's business he began progressively to under-
rate obedience to his parents. He returned with his
parents and submitted to them, in such a way that
he, who a little earlier had been shown, as God,
teaching the doctors among the Jews, is now shown,
as man, obeying even his earthly parents, giving us as
precise an example as we would wish of humility and
reverence". But such a sign of submission, says
St Ambrose, is not a sign of weakness. Rather is it
a sign of filial piety.

We are, however, at present considering the person and the exemplary conduct of Joseph, both to

see what we can learn for our own lives, and, insofar as we can, to establish certain facts (although they may not be mentioned explicitly). And these incontrovertible facts are that Joseph was head of the family and so had authority; that, as head of the family, he was obliged to educate Jesus; and that to this end he had to exercise that authority, teaching and correcting when necessary. At the same time as this, of course, he had to provide sustenance for the family.

Authority and Education

Expressed in this way it seems as if everything would have been fairly straightforward. But when one looks into it a little more attentively, and gives it some thought, it is not difficult to see that Joseph's was a delicate task and not one of little responsibility.

Beginning with perhaps his most obvious charge, the provision of sustenance, there is a vast difference between what is necessary and what is superfluous, if by what is necessary we understand not simply what is needed for survival but what a child needs to develop in his environment. With a poor family, the level of what is necessary cannot be very high. And so there is little danger of not educating the children properly through 'spoiling' them and satisfying their whims. But when the family standard of living is higher, and the economic means abound, this is a great danger. For the children cheerfully spend what they have not earned. They create superfluous, often harmful, needs which later on they will only be able to satisfy with doubly serious and constant work. Both abundance in the family and the ease with which they can receive money from their parents does not incline them to such work. There is, moreover, the harm which lack of responsibility and inadequate knowledge of the value of money bring in their wake in the long run. For the value of money can only be appreciated by those who earn it with effort.

This was not a great problem for Joseph, nor is it one for a great majority of parents. But it is helpful to realise this and to bear it in mind.

The education of children is an essential goal of matrimony and it is both a duty and a right for parents. A duty implies that it cannot be shaken off by the simple procedure of taking the children to a place where they receive education. Attendance at such institutions does not exonerate the parents from what they can do in the home. The home environment is so critical for educating the children that there can be no substitute for it. A right implies that no one can legitimately prevent the education of children or prevent a free choice of a school. Nor can anyone force parents or teachers to educate children in falsehood. And parents have to defend this right against the State or against whoever tries to wrest away from them the exercise of their obligation. It is they who will have to answer for their children before God. And it is this imperative that confers on them the right to educate.

Man is made in the image and likeness of God. He is gifted with reason, capable of knowledge, and a will free to love or not to love, to choose one thing or another, or to abstain from choosing. Education, then, will be directed principally to the development of the intellect and will. As the object of reason is truth, to educate the intellect is to seek and to accept the truth always, and never falsehood. As the object of the will is in the good, to educate it means to train it (if one may use such a graphic word) so that it wants what it ought to, in preference to its likes and dislikes. But it is a matter of effectively wanting, according to a relevant point in *The Way* (no. 316): "You tell me, yes, that you want to. Very good: but do you want to as a miser longs for gold, as a mother loves her child, as a worldling craves for honours, or as a wretched sensualist seeks his pleasure? No? Then you don't want to."

The father's duty to educate is clear. And if one wants to educate, one has to command. Obviously it will not be like an officer with his soldiers. We can't imagine Saint Joseph barking out orders. An indication is sufficient if he who commands has authority. It is those who don't have it who generally have to shout and even to threaten. Children ought not to rebel against or pay scant heed to these 'indications', although at times they disobey by putting off 'till later' what they ought to do. And the authority which one has in principle should be maintained. In this respect Sigrid Undset's observation from experience is important. "I have come to a further conclusion" she writes. "It is that parents have a duty to live in such a way that children can venerate them." Much earlier, another woman — St Teresa — in very different circumstances and manner, reached the same conclusion. "I sometimes think what harm is done by parents who do not always try to ensure that their children see always all kinds of virtues." There is a moral authority which not only inspires respect, but obedience too, and even docility. And this is much more important for a father than his ability to earn a lot of money. Exemplary in conduct and disposition, he should give a genuine and sympathetic attention to the progress and problems of his children (not show a mere condescension towards them as if patronising them with a casual and insignificant half-interest), and be considerate even in the way he deals with them; these are the elements that determine moral authority.

Parents and Their Children

Bernanos, with typical wit, makes a passing reference to the education of children in *Dialogues with the Carmelites* — a reference which is necessary to make the point. After a brief dialogue, one of the speakers ends with this great truth "it is easier to be a friend than a parent . . .".

And so it is. To be a friend rather than a parent is a lot easier, involving less work and no loss of sleep. To be a parent, to know how to be one, is a task that demands dedication, study (not just from books but of children), sensitivity, time, finesse and in a special way, much love and awareness of responsibility. Today it is difficult to be a parent. The concept of parental authority has been undermined to such an extent that it has even been presented as an obstacle to the liberty of children, a shackle to their free development. How does one get it right? If one is a parent 'of the old school', of 'orders and commands', of punishments, the children can end up rebelling and breaking away. To avoid this break, one compromises. The children can then 'blackmail' their parents into permitting them to live as they like, unfettered, with no discipline, so that the parents give in to everything under this kind of Damocletian sword. They swing between anguish and annoyance, not knowing whether it is better to continue giving in or to adopt a firmer and more energetic attitude.

The sad part of this problem is that there are no panaceas. Fortunately, though, there are some

principles. The parents should at least know there
are some things which depend on them and others
which do not. The latter should be entrusted to God
and left aside. For no matter how much such issues
are pondered and acted upon, the parents will be able
to do little, as these issues are beyond their competence. But in those things that do depend on
parents, they ought to concern themselves, and seriously so. As they are not owners of their children
(but rather like delegates from God to help their
children become men), to respect their freedom is as
important as making them respect their neighbour.
And an important aspect of this education in freedom is to let them assume responsibility. This pre-
supposes allowing them to face the consequences of
their actions.

The duty of parents is to educate them in the Law
of God and to teach them a role, as has been seen
earlier. As far as the first is concerned, the truths
necessary for salvation (necessary also in order to
live at peace in the world) should be the most important objective of education. For if there is no fear of
God, there is no guarantee for anything. And if their
lives unfold on a basis of untruths, then this life can
become rotten and wretched. Moreover, it can place
their eternal salvation in jeopardy. So the parents
have "to educate them in the law". The second duty
refers to placing them in conditions where they can
honourably earn a living and form a home. But this
should be done with respect for the aptitudes, incli-
nations and tastes of the children concerned; advis-
ing them is preferable to imposing our wishes on
them (for it is very hard to see them having to work
all their lives against the grain). Parents should not
confuse incentives (a carrot for the donkey?) with
rewards for laziness and lack of willpower.

Grace and Freedom

Joseph, of course, never experienced such problems or difficulties with Jesus. He did meet very difficult ones in other fields. And perhaps here is the clearest lesson, and even the most practical and sure one, we can deduce. For as far as education was concerned, Joseph did in each and every moment what he ought to have done, not what was more effective in order to obtain this or that result, nor what provided the easiest approach to achieve what he considered best. It is very important to stop here, if only for a moment. One cannot convert the obligations of parents into a riddle or a puzzle: 'how does one hit upon the right answer?'. For it is neither a game of chance they are playing, nor a stratagem they employ 'to obtain results'. Not the former — 'to guess' — because the exercise of authority or adopting the adequate means can never be entered into blindly. It is not a simple question of luck, but of maturity, of prudence, of integrity. Not, either, a result-motivated scheme because an effect is not, nor can it be, an objective but a consequence. The objective is to do what one ought to do, be it pleasing or not, comfortable or not. For if in looking for a result one does what one ought not to do, or omits doing it, it is difficult for anything not to turn out badly. Failure in duty never ends well. Just as important is for prudence to dictate how or when a thing is to be done. To ignore without correcting what is bad for fear of the reaction is cowardice, not prudence, and a way of endangering someone for whom we only want good.

For the same reason it is important, educationally, not to place at the same level what is essential and what is merely accidental. For with the former, any leeway could be disastrous, but in the latter case no departure from authoritative rigidity is deformative and quite likely to awaken feelings of irritation. The most appropriate means for children progressively to acquire maturity, (a process which ought to accompany growth), will be to help them develop an ever-increasing scope for personal initiative and the capacity to choose, inculcating in them a sense of proportion and allowing them to handle the consequences which their decisions bring in train.

In summary: parents ought to exercise authority if they want to educate; but they have to know how to exercise it. They have to fulfil their task of teaching, correcting and punishing when it is the only way to avoid harm: understanding, exacting, helping and forgiving; but always with the highest regard for freedom. With this regard for freedom they can see the limit to which they ought to go and from what point they ought to leave the child to take decisions and carry the consequences himself. But realising that education and example do not produce magical results, it is not enough to teach children if they do not wish to learn, nor generally is it enough to know what is good in order actually to do it. There is a great mystery in this delicate and tangible relationship between grace and freedom, and no one can ever guarantee the final result of a child's education. And so, perhaps, the most reasonable approach on the parents' part, in addition to using the human means, is to have sufficient humility to ask God for light and help in this tremendous undertaking.

18

The Son of the Craftsman

At the end of the episode of the finding of the Child Jesus in the Temple, St Luke says that Jesus "went down with them and lived at Nazareth". It appears as though Joseph spent all his life there, in Nazareth. "And what had life to offer someone from a forgotten village like Nazareth? Nothing but work: work every day, with the same constant effort. And at the end of the day, a poor little house in which to rest and to regain energy for the following day" (Mgr Escrivá).

This was, in effect, the life of Saint Joseph after his return from Egypt, just as it had been earlier, since the time he had become an adult. He probably died before Jesus began his public life, but he is still remembered in Nazareth some time later. And he is remembered, above all, for his occupation as a worker. The references in the Gospel confirm this.

"Jesus had now reached the age of about thirty. He was, by repute, the son of Joseph" (Luke 3:23). So says the evangelist when, having dealt with the baptism of Jesus, he opens the account of the public life with his genealogy. A little later, St Luke records the comment of the people, surprised as they were by the wisdom of his words: "Is this not the son of Joseph?" (Luke 4:22). This was on the occasion of a visit Jesus made to Nazareth, from which so little fruit resulted because of the incredulity of his fellow villagers.

This time St Luke takes Joseph's side, while it is St Matthew who mentions Our Lady. "Is this not the carpenter's son, whose mother is called Mary?" (Matt 13:55). St Mark, for his part, coincides more with St Matthew than St Luke. "Is not this the carpenter, the son of Mary?" (Mark 6:3).

A word of warning, however: the translation is not entirely accurate in using 'carpenter' as much with respect to Joseph as to Jesus. 'Faber' says the Latin Vulgate, a term usually translated as 'craftsman'. For Joseph was a man who had acquired skills in a craft or a trade, a worker who earned his living for himself and his family with his hands. St Justin is probably the source for identifying Saint Joseph's manual job with that of a woodworker, for so he says in his *Dialogue with Triphon*. Taking into account his authority and the fact that he wrote in the second century, it is not surprising that such a view has prevailed. But the term used in the Greek text can just as well signify a man working in iron as one who works in wood. Saint Ambrose, as well as Saint Hilary, refers to Joseph as a metalworker, and they are not the only ones. Anyway, it is not at all unlikely he was both. Nazareth, after all, was not such a large town as to have, let us say, specialist trades.

And as happens in little towns, rather than learning 'a trade', one learnt to tackle practical problems that cropped up in everyday life. One learnt to remedy or to satisfy the more urgent needs of the plain people of a simple village. Which is to say that there would be occupations which meant making and mending in different fields. There would be few 'demarcation disputes' in such a place in those days. There are those who translate the Greek as 'cabinetmaker' or 'builder of houses', and even an early author who makes him — with not much reason, to tell the truth — a silversmith.

In any event, whatever he was, his occupation was, without any doubt, of a humble nature and not prominent. "He was a workman who supplied the needs of his fellow citizens with a manual skill, acquired through years of toil and sweat" (Mgr Escrivá).

The Dignity of Work

He was the head of a family and a poor man. As head of a family, the responsibility of maintaining his dependants properly fell on him. Being a poor person he had no capital other than the expertise of his job. It was capital which had to provide its yield through work. And this is how Joseph has traditionally been seen, among tools and filings and shavings, forthright and honest at his bench, engaged in straightforward and uncomplicated tasks — which is not the same as what is easy. He persevered all his days in the same work, as if a certain piece of advice from Ecclesiasticus (11:21) had been self-imposed. It says: "Be constant in your job. Live at it, and grow old in your profession". His was a whole life spent working joyfully and without stressing unduly what was a continual service not only, albeit principally, to Jesus and Mary but in everything his small community required of him. It was a service provided by his skill and effort.

As with St Paul years later, Joseph did not receive his daily bread free. He toiled day and night so as not to be a burden on anyone (II Thess 3:8). He begged of no one. He brought up his tiny family with the bare necessities. That much is certain. He never overcame poverty but he had what was sufficient. And he did not limit himself to the mechanics of making things, of fulfilling orders. There are ways and ways of working. For work can be done with resentment, with indifference and almost mechanically, with little or no interest. But it can also be done joyfully. Generally speaking, only work done cheerfully is good work, for such work is done with love. There is great dignity in work. And this dignity — as Mgr Escrivá remarked — "is founded on love". It is love for work well done that is capable of giving distinction to the humblest of jobs . . . and to the person who carries it out.

As work was the activity to which Jesus was dedicated for the greater part of his life, it was sanctified by him and endowed with a redemptive value. Consequently it is capable of transcending purely natural limits and of converting itself into an offering to God. What is even more, it can come to mean cooperating in the work of redemption — on condition however, that it is really done with love. For it is this love that plucks work away from the weight of drudgery that can drag a man down. Love converts work into service. It is when care is taken to do a job well that one can speak with propriety about work as being honourable. Charles Peguy wrote some splendid pages on such 'honour'. Much of what he said is worth transcribing even if the quotation becomes a little extensive:

"We know the value of work. We have all seen care carried to perfection, present in the whole just as in the most intricate of details. We have known the piety of this 'work well done' carried to the most extraordinary degree . . . . Those workers . . . were men of repute. It was necessary for the leg of a chair to be well made. This was something clearly understood. It was to show excellence. It was not something to be done well for the sake of. . . wages. It had not to be done well for the sponsor, for the connoisseurs, nor for the clients of the sponsor. It was necessary to do it well for its own sake, in itself, by itself, in its very being. In this matter a deep tradition flows down to us from earlier generations, a history, an absolute. It used to be an honour, in the interest of all, that this chair leg be well made. Each leg, although it would be out of sight, was as perfect as if it were in view. This is the highest principle underlying the building of the great cathedrals. . . . All the other virtues are in accord with this one. Decency and refinement in language; respect for the home; a sense of respectful regard, respect of all kinds, self-respect. Everything was a constant ceremony. Frequently, on the other hand, the atelier was an extension of domestic ceremonial. The home was one with the workshop, and the honour of the home was identified with the honour of the place of work. . . . The rhythm of hearth and handicraft were as one ceremonial from the first light of day. Tradition and training were all important; everything had been handed down; everything went to build up and reinforce a healthy custom. Everything tended to raise up the heart and the mind, everything was a day-long prayer; sleeping and waking, work and brief rest, the bed and the table, the soup and the meat, the house and the garden, the open door and the street, the farmyard and the threshold to the home, and the meal on the table. . . . And as a consequence, the splendid affiliated and derived sentiments. Respect for the elderly, for parents, for the family. An admirable regard for children. Naturally, respect for the woman — and it is necessary to say this, for today one really misses respect towards a woman, in herself. A regard for the family and the home. And above all, the respect and pleasure in having respect itself; a respect for tools and for our hands, the supreme implements . . . . ."

While Peguy wrote *L'argent* (from which these quotations are taken) in 1912, and it could seem that his words fitted neither Joseph's time nor our own, there are some observations that deserve comment. In his childhood he still remembered craftsmen working in their own homes. Home and workshop were indeed one. A craftsman, of modest means, but independent, was not subject to a patron. He generally worked on orders placed with him personally; Saint Joseph appears to have been such a one. He carried out a variety of tasks; he made objects for different uses. He worked on them from the start until they were completely and properly finished. His life was "simple, normal and ordinary. It consisted of years of exactly the same work, of days which, one after the other, humanly speaking were monotonous" (Mgr Escrivá). But there were also new elements, because each day has its own special way of finding God in the work of that particular day for no two days can be exactly the same. It is the awareness of working in the presence of God that makes the difference between work, however good it may be, and work which, in addition to being good, transcends the natural limits through means of sanctification.

Sanctity Through Work

The work of the craftsman — the work of those to whom hurry does not seem to be synonymous with the task — is work done without impatience, without rushing; it is work done calmly. In a word, a piece of work done well without skimping time; for the best way is not always the shortest route, but at times may be the longest. And Joseph had all the time in the world. What did not seem to appeal to him was the desire to produce in quantity to earn a lot, at the cost of a defective and hurried job. He had what was needed and neither he nor Our Lady sought after anything else. In this way he gave the guidelines for acquiring the christian virtue of poverty, a standard which Mgr Escrivá has formulated for today's mentality in one of the points in *The Way* (no. 631): "Detach yourself from the goods of the world. Love and practise poverty of spirit: be content with what enables you to live a simple and sober life". And so, perhaps, it is easier for the man who is not over-ambitious to do his work well: he holds it in sufficient esteem not to burden himself with it; he can take care of the details and leave it well finished.

If a job is humble, if it is not eye-catching or not appreciated, it does not matter. The most exquisite products can be the least necessary for most people, and tend to be the most superfluous. To make bread is more necessary and lends greater service than to design jewelry. A wardrobe is more useful than a porcelain statuette. And it is no criticism of the artist-craftsman that any home can do without a lamp of cut glass more easily than without a table.

Certainly, men consider some jobs to be noble and others to be somehow inferior; they contrast between liberal work and servile work, between intellectual work and manual work. But it is also certain that in God's eyes it is other things that count. For "since Christ took it into his hands, work has become for us a redeemed and redemptive reality. Not only is it the background of man's life, it is a means and a path of holiness. It is something to be sanctified and something which sanctifies" (Mgr Escrivá). This is why the author of these words, Mgr Escrivá, states that he measures the effectiveness of a piece of work by its results insofar as it helped sanctify the person who carried it out. (It is to him that we can attribute the most fruitful clarification of work's being a christian vocation and also of its most beautiful consequences). One cannot, therefore, leave aside another important and enlightening consequence. It is to realise that the value of a job does not lie in its falling into one class or another, but in the love one puts into it, in the love with which one does it. In this light, a good carpenter is of greater standing than a bad teacher, and the work of a charlady can be, before God, more valuable than that of a Cabinet minister. Beneath the external coarseness of some jobs there is an inner nobility which can pass unnoticed by the eyes of men. But it is not missed by the loving eyes of God, who can see farther, and has a different way of measuring things and of evaluating both human work and man's other human activities.

For us, ordinary men who carry out ordinary work throughout our lives; for the women who toil one day after another in the same humdrum tasks, carried on with the same rhythm, ever unapplauded, as if nothing they ever did had the least importance; for those labourers who pour with sweat and of whom nobody takes the slightest notice since their work lacks glamour and prominence; for all those of us who carry out a hidden and unshining toil, the work of Joseph, the craftsman of an insignificant hamlet is an example and a consolation. "Can anything good come out of Nazareth?" (John 1:46). Christianity's answer to the unworthy question is Saint Joseph.

His work was neither comfortable nor brilliant, but thanks to it that little family was able to make progress. It was repetitive, with no great horizons, with no masterly products for later ages to admire, but he did not waver in constancy, nor in patience nor in daily effort. He was not unsettled, nor was he discontented with his work, changing constantly from one place of work to another, permanently dissatisfied. Nor did he seek in changes of jobs a calmness not to be found outside oneself, for when one does not love work, it is not possible to find any other kind of satisfaction in it, no matter how often one tries to turn to something else. And work is not easy to love if its reference to God and God's plans is missing.

It is true that it is not always possible to 'feel' satisfaction when a job is being done. Often perhaps one can offer to God no more than one's fatigue, the tiredness that constant effort — the work of each day, always the same — produces in us. We may not be able to experience the attraction of novelty, or the incentive that our work is something whose value will in the end come to be appreciated. Our exhaustion may not be glorious, as is, for example, that of a sportsman at the end of an event; our weariness will often have as little glory as the work which causes it. It does not matter. Joseph of Nazareth went through all of this, and no doubt had to overcome, like any other worker, the personal frustrations inseparable from his wrestling with stubborn materials. Jesus too knew the enervation and fatigue of a workshop, and the monotony of days with no prominence and no dramatic history. And with all of this, never was there a more fruitful work than that of Joseph.

The great Lope de Vega in his play dealing with the birth of Christ and the flight into Egypt, was able to highlight one of its more important aspects which has attracted less attention than it deserves.

Angel: A thousand times Blessed be
      Your divine and holy humility,
      For raising Joseph in all dignity
      When lowly and humble he seemed to be.
Jesus: He sustains my life,
      On his account I live,
      He governs and protects me.
      Joseph my legal father
      Takes this pre-eminence upon himself
      He comes to give sustenance
      To one who is universal sustenance itself.
      The earth owes to Joseph
      The blood I will give it
      For it came from his work.
Angel: May the heavens bless your name!
Jesus: The blood with which I was born,
      This is due to Mary.
      That which I use each day,
      This I owe to Joseph.

This is a daring and striking thought about man's labour and its tremendous significance for the continuance and development of human life. Peguy was right when speaking about work. "Teachers, priests and parents, tell us that a man who works well and who knows how to comport himself can be sure he will never lack what he needs." In these two requirements lie both the dignity of the poor — in working well and knowing how to behave — and the power of that dignity. Saint Joseph, it is true, never was the kind who could be called 'a successful man'. Anxiety for success can possibly become an obstacle to working well, when what can only really be a by-product is turned into an end in itself. It does not seem that this could ruffle Joseph's calm. It never came into his head that a lifelong stay in his humble condition could be something bad, or that lack of ambition to scale the steep and slippery slope of worldly advancement was a defect.

Perhaps the judgement of men would mark down Joseph as a failure for having spent a whole life and not prospered, and for not having had during his working life — if at any stage he had aspired to them — what may be known as 'creative prospects' or 'a promising career'. But this sort of criterion, not at all uncommon in our world, is a mistaken one, for Joseph achieved both objectives — not, of course, in the way men generally understand these expressions, but in another way, altogether distinct, because it is unconventional, but real. His 'creative prospects' were the promise of eternal life, the way of sanctity, and his 'career' developed such a brilliant future that the universal Church now has him as its patron. With Jesus and Mary he has merited forming the earthly trinity.

19

A Faithful and Prudent Servant

In the entry antiphon of the Mass of Saint Joseph on the 19th of March we read "He is a faithful and prudent servant. The Lord will entrust his family to him".

This is not one of those long texts which open up a multitude of horizons, complex and full of suggestions. On the contrary, it has just two brief sentences, each very clear and with a deep meaning. And these are not only for consideration and reflection, but also for application to real life today.

"A faithful and prudent servant." Who is a faithful and prudent servant? A servant is one who serves, who is of service, but one who in a certain way belongs to the master whom he serves, whatever that master's title to ownership really be. It is in this sense that Joseph 'served', as a man who had given himself to the service of God. His service was not in any sense as a slave, because in slavery there is a certain inhuman element — the slave is not free. Joseph was always free and he exercised his freedom by serving God voluntarily, when he knew God's will. He gave his life to God, not losing it through death as a martyr does, but dedicating it to the mission for which he had been called by God himself.

He was faithful because he always protected the faith due to his God and Master. Perhaps, with reference to Joseph, we could recall the concept of fidelity which was so highly developed in the Middle Ages: it meant a personal relationship of loyalty and attachment to the 'lord'; a firmness, without flaw, in keeping one's word or a promise given, come what might and in spite of any inconvenience, difficulties or obstacles that might present themselves. Fidelity, then, had an image (perhaps it would be better described as a property) which inspired and gave confidence. A faithful man is one who is steady in the faith given to him: a man, in short, on whom one can rely.

And he was wise, for he always worked with prudence. To work with prudence is to be able to discern, to know how, in considering a course of action, to distinguish what is good from what is not. But this is not all. There is more to it than that. A prudent man is, above all, one who is capable of knowing reality and of not departing from it. He is thus a man who relies on a solid basis of principle in coming to decisions. Joseph, in effect, does not appear to have been in that class of men who set about all their activities, or at least the greater part of them, by planning projects which are never-ending, because, among other reasons, they have never been properly begun. He did not belong to that class of men who dream of great things, and, while thus immersed, let slip the specific duties which ought to be fulfilled step by step at each moment. These duties are more real than all the marvellous but imaginary projects in which they are so caught up. Joseph, as a prudent man, did not build unsubstantial dreams, but took his decisions on the basis of the precise data with which the reality of life furnished him.

Joseph as a Servant

Here we have a man with a clear realisation of his condition as a servant with respect to his God and Lord, a man who by this very fact knows that his mission is to serve God and wants to do so freely and deliberately. He is a man who, precisely because he has accepted his position with full deliberation and with total freedom, remains faithful to his decision to the point of holding firm in spite of all setbacks or dangers. Being prudent, and thus aware of the realities of life, he is capable of making the resolution appropriate to each case or set of circumstances without being misled by harebrained optimism, blind ambition or silly vanity. He is, then, a man worthy of confidence.

Joseph was such a man, for "the Lord entrusted his family to him". God relied on him, leaving in his care his Incarnate Son and his Blessed Mother — the two greatest treasures that could possibly have been entrusted to any creature. For to entrust is to rely on another, surely and immoveably. It consists in leaving something valuable in his charge with no guarantee of its safe keeping other than the certainty which his proven fidelity provides. God knew he was faithful and prudent, and so He made him — as that happy phrase has it — "his right hand man". Here is a class of man in whose loyalty one can repose with complete serenity. He will not fail however bad things are; he will remain loyal through any contradictions that might arise, and will be able to bring to a conclusion, in the way he should, the things entrusted to him.

Nothing deflected Joseph from the way that had been pointed out to him. No stumbling block, no threat, no peril could break down or even diminish his fidelity. Nor did he give in to the temptation (very attractive at times) to venture onto a treacherous slope whose incline is scarcely perceptible and end up justifying, under the pretext of being more useful, a lack of faithfulness with the excuse of being then in a position to lend a more effective service. Joseph was a man who maintained his position and subordinated all legitimate ambition to the mission entrusted to him. It would seem that he had no desire or ambition other than that of serving.

Consequently, the Church could well choose and use for the antiphon of the Mass of the 19th of March those words from the parable of the talents selected by Matthew for his Gospel: "Enter, good and faithful servant, into the joy of your Lord" (Matt 25:21).

For a prudent and faithful servant is a good servant; he is a servant who works for good. He works, not occasionally or accidentally, as if by exception, but habitually, in an ordinary way, as effect follows cause. And the cause in this case is goodness. A man is good because the quality of his work is such that from it only good comes: it is like a good tree that gives good fruit.

What else was his life if not a total dedication to the service for which he had been called? Husband to Our Lady, legal father to Jesus (he was much more than this, but it is necessary to qualify the noun to avoid misunderstanding, although the Gospel does not use such an adjective, and makes room for reflection). He devoted his life to the attention he paid them, dedicated to fulfilling his vocation — the mission to which he had been called. As a dedicated man is one who does not belong to himself, Joseph stopped being concerned for himself from the moment when, enlightened by an angel in that first dream, he fully accepted God's designs for him. Receiving Mary as his spouse he began to live for those who had been placed in his care. God had entrusted him with his family, and Joseph did not disappoint him. God sought support in him, and he stood firm in every instance. He was not assigned to a brilliant role (in the sense in which it is usually understood) but this did not matter to him. And he made the same effort to carry out his unseen tasks as he would have done in fulfilling any other service on which God might have employed him.

Thus it was that a man who was straightforward, a hard worker, patient, long suffering, willing to serve, quiet, humble, obedient and simple was praised as a just, faithful, prudent and good man. He is recognised as an effective man who knew, in difficult circumstances, how to lead forward the family God had placed in his care, protecting it and keeping it free from dangers. And he did all this without giving it exceptional importance, without becoming conceited at the confidence placed in him, with neither complaints nor protests, without a single gesture of dissent in those perplexing and difficult times through which, incomprehensible to human eyes, God made him live. Nothing favourable or adverse would change his loyalty to God or his dedication to the service of Jesus and Mary. So constant was he in his day-to-day business that if ever a man could truly, and in all justice, be called faithful, that man was Joseph of Nazareth.

A Sense of Service

If the Church applies the qualification of servant to Joseph, if she calls "Servants of God" men who have died with the fame of sanctity, then to be a servant, a person willing to serve, a man who gives himself in the service of others, ought not to be in itself as contemptible as it generally sounds to our super-civilized contemporary ears. To be in service is held to be somehow menial and tends to be looked down upon. There is something pejorative in the way a person who serves is thought of, unless he serves the State, a business, or something as vague or impersonal as an institution. To serve another man, or a family or other men, is seen to involve a certain humiliation, something inferior, which places a man who does serve on a level some degree below human dignity.

Nevertheless, Jesus himself said that he had come to serve, not to be served (Matt 20:28). He served his own disciples to show them this. Our Lord went on his knees before them and washed their feet. "An example I have given you" (John 13:5), he told them, commanding them to serve one another. To serve, then, is not to do something demeaning, to cringe; nor is it in any way beneath human dignity. The condition of a servant does not bear any kind of stigma, nor is to serve any sort of humiliation. Joseph of Nazareth did nothing except to serve his own with his person and his neighbours with his work. Of no unusual significance or extraordinary importance, this work of his, not even remarked upon when Joseph appears in the gospel narratives, is nevertheless for him what their own special work ought to be for all men — at once a means of livelihood and the formative road they travel through life. His daily task, the craft he laboured at, formed the life that was Joseph's.

Service is not servility. The two are distinct. But the difference between the two concepts is perhaps to be sought within each of them — the idea, as it were — and not externally in a purely linguistic way. A mother does not feel humbled through having to serve her own children, or a wife to serve her husband. When one loves, service is not laborious. If it is as St Augustine said, then the very work itself is loved. When one sees in one's neighbour the image and likeness of God, to serve him does not and cannot humiliate. When one does a job joyfully, the question does not even arise. No professor, for example, who is one by vocation, thinks he is rendering anything but a service when he gives a lecture or speaks with his students. Servility, on the other hand, is born when one believes himself to be so great that he cannot possibly serve others. Such a one would think himself debased by lowering himself in the eyes of his inferiors. Nevertheless, out of self-interest or because he is obliged, he serves, when he does so, against his will. Neither the humble person nor one who is in love is servile. Only the egoist, the self interested or the proud man can become servile.

It is not easy for the head of a family to be equal to his duty if he is not willing to serve his own unselfishly, to seek above all their good and this at his own expense. He must not see himself as being humbled merely because service to one's own involves giving over the necessary time to the family, even though such service might also imply cutting back somewhat on friends, entertainment and social or business arrangements.

Today not even those of us who call ourselves christians — which is to say disciples of Christ — seem very much inclined to the virtue of humility. Perhaps this is the reason for the much lamented deterioration of standards in so many trades and professions which are carried on without love, without a spirit of service, without any real care for 'doing a good job'. A christian ought to know that he is no more than his Master. And if Jesus said he had come not to be served but to serve, then to be the servant of others ought to be what christians aspire to. We have an obligation towards those whom God has put in our care. It is easy to see why John Paul II, in the homily of that Mass with which he opened his pontificate exclaimed: "Oh Christ! Let me be made a servant, and allow me to remain one . . . Make me a servant!"

Prudence and Faithfulness

What then of prudence? It seems as though this virtue, as well as patience, is considered peculiar to the aged, as if these were examples of residual virtues, virtues that feebly remain in those who because of their advanced years are timid and lethargic and cannot practise the more brilliant virtues of courage, magnanimity, fortitude. . . . This is false, of course. Prudence, like patience, or meekness, or any of the virtues which one may feel to be less attractive or even a little passive, do not indicate old age or senility, but maturity. The imprudent father of a family will be quite immature, and also show himself to be below the standard required of his position.

The comedian may treat it as one, but matrimony is no joke; it is neither simply a remedy for concupiscence, nor a kind of legalised sentimental adventure. It demands a sense of responsibility, and consequently a prudence proper to maturity — which is none other than a true appreciation of reality. He who madly launches out into dubious projects, depending on luck, because he thinks that it is proper for men to run risks, shows not only a limited intelligence, but also very little consideration for his family. No one can legitimately set at risk the reasonable security that ought to be provided for a wife and children by cheerfully moving from one post to another, with the hope of improving a 'life-style', of earning more money, with no guarantee other than that of blind optimism. It isn't that one may not seek to improve one's position, but that one ought to procure it prudently; that it is to say, without taking unnecessary risks, without vague optimism and without leaving firm ground. There are always risks, but when, in addition, we embark on plans where the surest 'facts' are those which our imagination offers, it is important to ascertain what these plans can lead to. One cannot always be looking for more, more, more, in reference to earthly things, for it is only in the love of God that there ought not to be limits. Moreover, it can be a real tragedy for the relatives of such a man, when they can hardly be certain of anything except that any decision he makes will almost inevitably be premature and precipitate — typical traits of the imprudent.

As for faithfulness . . . it is the splendid crown of matrimony. St Thomas in his usual laconic way says: "It corresponds to the faithfulness of man in fulfilling what he has promised". Centuries earlier, St Jerome, commenting on Isaiah, characterised him as one who "fulfilled what he had promised". He carried out what he had said he would. Just as one does not build upon sand, since on such an insecure foundation there is no guarantee of stability, so to build up a family on the promise of a shallow, impetuous and changeable man could lead to serious consequences. For the family is something very important. It is the basic building-block cell of society. The very life of humanity depends on it. And the christian family is more — it is the "domestic church", the place where new christians are formed. It is a school of custom, of traditional mores in which children develop and until they are able to look after themselves. Naturally, to bring this task to fruition, the spouses have to be united; this they will be, provided they are faithful to the word they have given, to the promise they freely contracted. Can anyone trust a man who does not keep his word? If he is not faithful to the one woman he freely chose among many to be his wife, if he is unable to school himself in patience, sometimes curbing his own will for the sake of keeping his promise and in order to safeguard for his children a secure and peaceful home, how can he be relied upon to keep his word in any other context? What about those towards whom he has fewer obligations than he has to his wife or children?

Go to Joseph

"He was an ordinary sort of man whom God relied on to work wonders. He did exactly what the Lord wanted him to do in each and every event which went to make up his life. That is why Sacred Scripture praises Joseph, as a just man" (Mgr Escrivá). God relies on ordinary men to work great deeds. It is a splendid and noble thing to form men, and even more to participate in the formation of christians capable of serving God and their fellows. God wishes that ordinary men like Joseph will be able to assume their responsibilities, to serve with prudence and fidelity, to live all the facets of their lives in following His way. Then they will be, like Joseph, *just* men.

To whom but Joseph could God have entrusted the Holy Family? When St Francis of Assisi said that "we should never consider ourselves superior to others, but ought to serve every human being for God", it seems as if he was thinking about Joseph. Or St Thomas Aquinas, who quotes St Jerome to make his point about the fittingness of Our Lady's betrothal. She was betrothed, he says "so that Saint Joseph could serve her". The Roman Pontiffs and the Magisterium of the Church pronounce similarly on the place of Joseph in the economy of God's Providence. Mgr Escrivá, his devotion life-long, has written in the same vein and along the same lines. "Among the promoters of devotion to Saint Joseph in recent times he holds an eminent position" writes L. Herran. Mgr Escrivá earnestly advises us to turn to him whom St Teresa called "the great saint", with these words: "Master of the interior life, a worker deeply involved in his job, God's servant continually in contact with Jesus. That is Joseph. *Ite ad Ioseph.* With Saint Joseph, the christian learns what it means to belong to God and fully to assume one's place among men, sanctifying the world. Get to know Joseph and you will find Jesus. Talk to Joseph and you will find Mary, who always fills that attractive workshop in Nazareth with peace."

Other books, available in English, by the same author:

Mary of Nazareth

In this book Fr Suarez studies the life, character, thoughts and piety of Our Lady. He also compares her moral and religious attitude to our own, focussing special attention on certain areas — for instance, vocation in whatever state and condition we find ourselves. His deep analysis of all the gospel texts helps us to understand Our Lady from both the human and supernatural points of view. In this way she appears to us in the right perspective, as a privileged person to whom much was given but also from whom more was asked than any one else.

The Narrow Gate

Being a Christian involves listening to the word of God. And trying to live it — by a combination of faith and reason, grace and virtue. *The Narrow Gate* is a collection of addresses given by Fr Suarez to university students. With quiet, incisive and gospel-based advice, this book could be useful to everyone.

About Being A Priest

This is a book every priest should read. What appears powerfully is Fr Suarez's positive approach. He combines the highest idealism with sanctified common sense. It can be recommended to prospective candidates for the priesthood because it is clear, concise and very readable. It comes near to classical stature.